Your Essential Guide to Dental School Admissions

30 Successful Application Essays and Collective Wisdom from Young Dentists

Edited by Helen Yang, DMD

ACKNOWLEDGMENTS

This book would not have been possible without the advice, tips, and essays submitted by dozens of young dentists and soon-to-be-dentists. Very special and heartfelt thanks to the dentists on the selection committee for volunteering their time, hard work, and input.

I would like to thank Max M. for editing the draft and Heather D. for her profound knowledge on self-publishing. I'd also like to acknowledge my supportive parents. ("Don't waste time watching so much TV. Write a book or something.")

CONTRIBUTORS

Eric C. Chen, DDS

University of California Los Angeles School of Dentistry, 2016

University of California Los Angeles School of Dentistry, Orthodontics and Dentofacial Orthopedics Residency, 2019

> *Dr. Chen served as dental school Class President and Chair of UCLA's national award-winning Pre-Dental Outreach Committee. He is a member of the UCLA NIH R25 grant program with a focus on dental education and professional mentorship, and has previously staffed the American Dental Education Association Pre-dental Student Virtual Fair.*

Irina F. Dragan, DDS, MS

Carol Davila University Romania, 2009

Assistant Professor, Tufts University School of Dental Medicine

> *Dr. Dragan received her Certificate in Periodontology and Master of Science degree from TUSDM in 2015. Dr. Dragan has been practicing dentistry limited to the field of periodontology and implant dentistry at Tufts Faculty Practice, published clinical and educational research papers, and contributed to textbook chapters. She has been honored for her work, most recently in 2016 by the American Dental Education Association. She currently serves as the Program Director for the Dental Education Learning and Teaching Academy Fellowship to support dentists interested in an academic career.*

Lauren E. Kuhn, DMD

Harvard School of Dental Medicine, 2017

Medical University of South Carolina College of Dental Medicine, Endodontics Residency, 2019

Dr. Kuhn has mentored for pre-dental students for many years, including serving as the HSDM Pre-Dental Chair from 2013-2014. She completed a research project in dental public health in Uganda, presented lectures at the Iwate Medical University in Japan, and placed 4th runner-up in the 2015 Miss America Pageant.

Lisa Lian, DMD

Harvard School of Dental Medicine, 2016

Columbia University College of Dental Medicine, Pediatric Dentistry Residency, 2018

Dr. Lian served as National Secretary and Northeast Regional Representative for the American Dental Education Association. She is passionate about improving dental education through innovative teaching styles by incorporating technology, problem-based learning and research in the classroom.

Lily Liu, DMD

Harvard School of Dental Medicine, 2016

General Dentistry, Boston

While an undergraduate student in the Biomedical Science program at The Ohio State University, Dr. Liu conducted interviews and served on the admissions committee. She has edited essays for college, graduate, and postgraduate admissions. She completed an AEGD through the Lutheran/ Langone Medical Center program at Fenway Health and currently works in private practice.

Daryn Lu, DDS

University of Oklahoma College of Dentistry, 2015

General Dentistry, Oklahoma City

> *Dr. Lu's passion for the dental profession shows through his journey within organized dentistry. He currently serves on the boards of the Oklahoma County Dental Society, Oklahoma Dental Foundation, the Academy of General Dentistry Oklahoma chapter, and is a guest writer for the ADA New Dentist Now and igniteDDS blogs.*

Sangita Murali, MS

Tufts University School of Dental Medicine, DMD Candidate 2018

> *Sangita Murali has used her experiences in admissions interviewing as well as her experiences as an applicant who matriculated at a top-ranked dental school to guide dozens of applicants successfully through the dental school admissions process. She is passionate about creating supportive environments to empower pre-dental and current dental students through academic mentorship and oral health promotion in community outreach.*

Jason Watts, DMD

Nova Southeastern University College of Dental Medicine, 2015

General Dentistry, Lithia, FL

> *Dr. Watts served as Vice President of the American Student Dental Association from 2014-15. He owns a practice called "Watts Dental." He travels all over the country to speak to dental students and dentists about the business of dentistry, motivational speaking on vision building, negotiations, and economics of our profession. He has mentored dozens and spoken to thousands.*

TABLE OF CONTENTS

PREFACE

Each year, more than 11,000 aspiring pre-dents apply for admission to dental schools in the United States. The process is tremendously competitive, with some schools having acceptance rates as low as 5%. It is no longer enough to get above-average grades and DAT scores. How do you stand out and present a compelling case for why YOU should be accepted over someone with similar attributes and statistics?

The idea for this book as a resource "for pre-dents, by dentists" was conceived three years ago. In dental school, I helped applicants revise personal statements, conducted mock interviews, and even wrote a few letters of recommendation. I had the privilege of serving a term on my school's admissions committee and played a role in shaping the new class. Having learned about its inner-workings, I wanted to help more future applicants navigate this lengthy, complicated process.

Of all the components in an application, the personal statement seems to intimidate applicants most. After all, it's open-ended, so it's completely up to you to do justice to your experiences, hopes and dreams in just 4,500 characters. Difficult indeed.

My goal was to create a collection of well-written and successful dental school personal statements to help applicants like yourself brainstorm and find inspiration. Such a resource doesn't currently exist. Being an inveterate procrastinator, I didn't embark on this project until after graduation, faced with lots of free time at work. (My takeaways: You can't show up in a new community and expect patients to flock to your clinic. Use the downtime to learn. Get friendly with staff.)

Nine months ago, I assembled a thoughtful team of young dentists who have experience with admissions and passion for mentoring. We reached out to dental students across the country, inviting them to submit their own personal statements in original form. At first, I wasn't sure how this project would be received or if anyone would actually entrust strangers with their intimate works.

Within a few weeks, we received over fifty submissions, and the committee went to work. Each essay was blinded, reviewed by four readers, and scored for content, style, and overall effectiveness. There were many excellent submissions, from which we ultimately selected thirty winning essays, published here for the first time. Each essay is accompanied by commentary on why we found it compelling and effective, as well as the author's bio to give you a sense of the type of applicant he or she was.

These thirty young dentists and soon-to-be-dentists come from 25 different colleges and nine dental schools. Their undergraduate studies ranged from biomedical sciences to electrical engineering to film studies. While most applied to enter dental school right after college, several were non-traditional applicants with non-dental work experience or advanced degrees.

Indeed, even the best personal statement isn't enough to secure the coveted acceptance letter. In addition to the essays in Part II, the first half of the book consists of four chapters written by members of our selection team. They are full of real advice and strategies honed from having applied to dental school and in some cases having sat on the other side of the admissions table. Chapter 1 focuses on getting impactful letters of recommendation and extracurricular activities. Chapter 2 revisits the authoring of our own personal statements from a more analytical angle. Chapter 3 arms you with tips to put your best foot forward during interviews, and Chapter 4 takes a step back from the application cycle to look at the big picture.

The team and I are so excited to share this resource with you. We hope it truly serves as your essential guide to dental school admissions!

— *Helen Yang, DMD*

PART I

Chapter 1

ASSEMBLE AN OUTSTANDING APPLICATION

BY: ERIC C. CHEN, DDS AND HELEN YANG, DMD

AADSAS (short for Associated American Dental Schools Application Service) is the official application portal for U.S. dental schools.[1] The online application is divided into four sections:

1. **Background information:** Name, address, contact info, etc
2. **Academic profile:** Coursework, grades, and standardized testing scores
3. **Evaluations:** Letters of recommendation
4. **Experiences:** Extracurricular activities and achievements

By the time you reach the application stage, the information in sections 1 and 2 are mostly fixed and have little room for improvement or elaboration. Sections 3 and 4, on the other hand, contain opportunities to put your best, most strategic, foot forward. This chapter focuses on how to obtain your strongest letters of recommendation, how to make the most of your extracurricular activities, and ends with general application tips.

---

[1]Foreign-trained dentists interested in applying for two-year advanced standing programs use another portal called the ADEA Centralized Application for Advanced Placement for International Dentists.

Recommendation letters that make you stand out

On establishing mentor-mentee relationships:

Q) What is a mentor?

Strong letters of recommendation start with strong relationships. A mentor is both an advisor and a coach, your champion and your cheerleader. A mentor is someone who you trust, understands your goals, and is actively looking out for your best interests. The roles and responsibilities differ from relationship to relationship and are amenable to change over time. While some relationships are part of a structured program (a thesis advisor in college or dentist-mentoring program), other may be more informal (a coach, a dentist you've shadowed, or a student club's faculty advisor). Try to check in with your mentor periodically, ideally with in-person meetings. It's not about the quantity, but the *quality* of these interactions.

Q) How do I approach someone to be my mentor?

This process is best when organic. Asking someone directly "can you mentor me?" places a lot of pressure on the other individual to fulfill expectations. Instead, start with small, specific asks that the person can concretely help you with. First, when approaching someone, make sure you've done your homework; clearly articulate the guidance you are seeking and how they can help you. Your primary goal may be dental school, but there are secondary goals that mentors can help with, such as getting a research publication or exploring different health careers. Second, convey how much of their time you think you will need. Make it clear how much time and energy you are willing to invest into this relationship. After all, it's a two-way street! Third, know when to back off. If you sense that your potential mentor is unwilling or unable to commit to mentoring you, don't force it. Look elsewhere for someone who can be more available and committed at this time.

Q) Dental schools require a letter of recommendation from a science professor. How can I stand out if I only see them 1-3 times a week during lectures?

The simplest answer is, give them something to write about! If you plan to ask your organic chemistry professor who lectures to 500 students each semester, it's not enough to ace his class. You must make the extra effort to have some meaningful interactions with that individual, and they should be aware and supportive of your pre-dental aspirations. Indeed, the person you ask should not be caught off guard by your request!

Consider it from your professors' perspective: if all they remember about you is that you showed up to class, their letter will be impersonal and of limited help. However, if they know that you frequently attended office hours, asked intelligent questions that showed you were prepared, helped fellow classmates with lab work, struggled with the midterm but made a big comeback, etc, the letter will be meatier. Some science classes offer the opportunity for peer tutoring or helping out in lab. Seize opportunities during the semester to get to know your professors.

Furthermore, it may be strategic to invest your time getting to know a professor from the smaller science classes with more personal interactions or a professor who won't be receiving several dozens of requests for letters each spring. Remember, it's about maximizing the quality and impact of each letter.

How to Obtaining Your Glowing Letter:

Q) Who should I ask for a letter of recommendation?

It is wise to create a panel of letter writers who know you in different ways. Instead of asking only science professors whose classes you aced and dentists you've shadowed, try to include an English teacher, a coach, a spiritual leader, the director of the club you lead, or the manager at your job. Envision what their letters would look like; think about the different positive insights each letter can shed about you, whether it's your intellectual curiosity, your tenacity, or your reliability. Too often, admissions officers read three or four letters saying very similar, rather generic things about an applicant ("strong student," "respectful and pleasure to work with")—what a missed opportunity.

If you were heavily involved in research, it is generally expected to include a letter from your research mentor. Schools may consider it to be a red flag, for instance, if you did not include a letter from a research mentor despite working in their laboratory for two years.

It may be tempting to ask a department chair or someone famous for a letter. Only do this IF you actually had significant, meaningful interactions with this individual. Just because your letter writer is impressive does not mean their letter will show YOU to be impressive. Impersonal letters don't add much value and are quickly glossed over by admissions officers.

Q) What is the best way to ask?

If possible, ask for the letter in person rather than by email. By asking in person, you are guaranteed a response, favorable or not. Electronic messages may get lost amongst a sea of emails and you might not hear back from your potential letter writer for some time. In addition, make sure to ask whether the individual can write you a "strong letter" because a tepid or generic letter will not bolster your application.

It is possible that the person you asked will admit that they are unable to provide you with a strong letter or more likely, say they are too busy. Should this happen, try not be too disappointed. Rather, be thankful that they were honest and gave you the chance to find someone who can write a more positive letter.

Q) When is the best time to ask?

Give your letter writer a minimum of three weeks; any less time is impolite. The best time to ask is soon after a meaningful activity or class has concluded, so your interactions with the letter writer are fresh in his or her mind. If you really bonded with your sophomore year biochemistry professor and plan on asking her for a letter, ask for a letter at the conclusion of the class. This way, years later when you are ready to apply for dental school, the letter is ready to go and needs only minor updates.

If you are gearing up to apply for dental school and plan on asking someone with whom you haven't recently been in touch, it is a good idea to reach out and schedule an in-person meeting. Your mentor/letter writer will want to hear from you and hear about what you've been up to since your activity or class concluded. This can jumpstart your relationship and remind your mentor about your qualifications and motivations to pursue dentistry.

Q) How can I help the letter writer write me the strongest possible letter?

Your letter writers are likely writing letters for other applicants as well, so you should go above and beyond to make their job as easy as possible. Provide them with the following information:

- **Instructions** on how and where to submit the letter and deadline. If it needs to be mailed, provide a stamped envelope. If submitted online, provide an easy reference of the web links.

- **Updated curriculum vitae.** This should include awards, honors, recognitions, extracurricular activities and leadership positions, public service, volunteer activities, employment, and research experience.

- **An informal history of your interactions.** This is a HIGHLY effective technique! In the email or a separate document, provide short notes on the length of interaction you have with the letter writer/mentor, key encounters, what you've learned from them, and how you've grown in the time they have known you. This is essentially a letter's core information, so providing it for your recommender ensures your letter will be as specific as possible. In addition, it shows you to be a thoughtful and resourceful individual.

- **A draft of your personal statement**, if already written. It does not have to be completely polished, but providing a decent draft can help your recommender learn more about you and your motivations.

Q) How many letters should I submit?

Aim for four letters, unless there are special extenuating circumstances. Before adding a fifth letter, really consider if this letter can contribute new information or shed new light on you. It is important to review dental school-specific requirements regarding the number of and types of letters of recommendation. Some require two letters from science professors. Some schools encourage applicants to include a letter from a dentist; other schools require such a letter.

Some undergraduates offer pre-med/pre-dental committee letters that synthesize or excerpt the other letters of recommendation. If your college offers such a service, realize that the committee letter holds more weight than individual ones. Make an effort to get to know your pre-dental committee members in advance.

Q) How do I follow-up with my letter writers?

You may start developing feelings of urgency when waiting on that one final letter before your application is marked complete. Remember that the dentist you shadowed or your college organic chemistry professor are busier than you think! Allow 2-3 weeks to pass before reminding your letter writer. A tactful way is to send an email simply thanking them again for being able to write you a letter, and ask if there is anything you can do to help. In doing so, you are tactfully reminding without explicitly pestering them again. In the event that one of your letter writers falls through and either they are unable to submit your letter in time or you suspect they only have time to write a generic letter (thereby weakening your application), consider requesting a letter from someone else as a backup.

Extracurricular Activities and Awards

Admissions officers want to understand how you occupy your time outside of school, where your interests lie, and how you handle responsibility. AADSAS does not collect a resume; instead, it has individual sections for you to type in extracurricular activities, honors/

awards, and any job/technical certifications you may have. When it comes to what AADSAS calls "experiences," remember the theme of this chapter: quality over quantity!

Q) What is considered an extracurricular activity?

AADSAS divides experiences into following the following categories:

- **Academic enrichment.** Summer or after-school activities sponsored by colleges or non-profits. For example, Summer Health Professions Education Program, and the Loyola University Summer Medical and Dental Education Program.

- **Dental shadowing.** Time spent observing dentists at work. Try to shadow dentists in different work settings and specialties.

- **Employment.** Non-dental related jobs. Includes any full-time or part-time jobs, work-study, summer internships, paid tutoring or teaching assistant positions.

- **Extracurricular activities.** Examples include involvement in school clubs, professional associations, non-profit organizations, sport teams, music groups, etc.

- **Research.** Includes only projects not done for academic credit/class. Research does not necessarily involve laboratory science; you can get involved with projects in the humanities, social sciences, or engineering too.

- **Volunteering.** Participating in or organizing community service activities. Includes hospital or clinic volunteering, assisting at a homeless shelter, tutoring, organizing fundraisers for charities.

Q) How can I get more dentistry-related experiences?

Admissions officers are looking for evidence that you researched the dental profession. In addition to shadowing, here are some other activities to increase exposure to the field and show that you are serious about becoming a dentist.

- **Join a pre-dental club.** This is an excellent avenue to meet like-minded students and learn about the profession through club activities and lectures. If your school does not have such a club, even better, take the initiative to start your own!

- **Volunteer in a dental clinic.** Many communities have free/low-cost clinics. Volunteering there in any capacity presents opportunities to learn about access to care issues in dentistry.

- **Dental assisting.** Chair-side assisting is the next step up from shadowing. Some pre-dental students have worked part-time or over the summer assisting the dentist or office manager. Some states require dental assistants to be licensed, while others allow on the job learning, so check your local laws first.

- **Conduct research.** Dental research is an incredibly diverse field, ranging from oral microbiology to stem cell biology, from material sciences to biostatistics. Look for opportunities in local dental, medical, or graduate schools. If you do not live near research institutions, consider spending a summer doing research full-time. Another option is to email professors for potential projects that can be done remotely.

- **Go on a medical/dental service trip.** Look for opportunities to volunteer on an overseas missions trip organized by reputable organizations, dental societies, or dental schools. If you do choose to join, keep in mind what you can and cannot do. Since you're not yet a dentist, make sure the activities you engage in on the trip are appropriate given your role.

- **Join dental professional organizations.** Dental organizations are a great resource to meet dentists and dental students from across the country. The American Student Dental Association (ASDA) has a pre-dental membership category with publications and events created specifically for pre-dental students; you can join through their website at *www.asdanet.org*.

Q) How are activities and awards entered into AADSAS?

Experiences are entered one at a time and sorted in one of six above categories (academic enrichment, dental shadowing, etc). Awards and certifications go in separate sections. For each experience, you will list the name of the organization, the highest title held, total number of hours, average hours/week, and the dates of your participation. You are also given up to 600 characters (approximately 75 words) to describe your role and key responsibilities. Make the most of this space to share what you achieved and/or learned. Complete sentences are not necessary.

AADSAS lets you input maximum of six activities per category, and choose up to four achievements and six experiences to list on the application's cover sheet. Choose strategically to tell a narrative of what you can contribute to a dental school community. Are you artistic? Athletic? Analytical? A leader or a team player? Introverted or extroverted? Passionate about helping children with special needs, researching dental implants, or maintaining a YouTube channel? Think about the positive traits that admissions officers would look favorably upon, including dedication and passion for an activity/team/cause, initiative, ability to organize and execute, and interesting hobbies. Then, describe your activities in a way to highlight those positive attributes and make you stand out.

Q) How can I show an activity was meaningful/impressive?

Admissions officers want to see that you've engaged meaningfully with your activities and are wary of those who pad their resumes for the sake of the application or list a large number of activities only for a short time. Quality can be demonstrated in the following ways:

- **Length of time.** Activities that you consistently participated in over several years are more impressive than activities done for one semester. Keep that in mind when considering which activities to stop as you become busier over time. It may be more strategic to remain involved, albeit less so, than quitting an activity entirely.

- **Total number of hours.** You will be asked to input the total number of hours of participating in an activity. A high number signals greater investment and can be impressive. However, be prepared to talk about these more substantial activities in detail in the interview. After all, it would be a red flag if you claim to have volunteered in a hospital for 200 hours but cannot elaborate on it in person (what you learned, why you enjoyed it).

- **Growth.** Showing progress or advancement in an activity is looked upon favorably. An example would be starting as a general member in the Pre-dental Club, and later becoming elected to the board or even President.

- **Results and achievements.** Activities through which you may have won statewide or national recognition, for example, demonstrate your aptitude and excellence. Other ways to impress with your extracurriculars include spearheading a major project, organizing successful large events or fundraisers, presenting a research project at a national conference, creating a publication or website, or any number of achievements.

- **Break new ground.** Instead of following the status quo, brainstorm and implement a new project of your own, whether it's founding a new student group, starting a publication, organizing an event that's the first of its kind on campus, or something that shows your creativity and independence.

- **Confirmation from letter writers.** Another voice besides your own to vouch for your accomplishments and dedication can lend additional weight to the activity.

Q) What if I have relatively few activities to show for?

First, relax in knowing that you likely are more multi-faceted than you think, even if you avoided organized activity like the plague. AADSAS recognizes a wide range of activities, from summer jobs to sports to hobbies. Your hobbies can be listed under Extracurricular activities, especially if they are unique or feature manual dexterity. Furthermore, the dental shadowing you've done shows up first on the application summary.

Second, there are a few ways to improve upon this weakness in a short time period. Hopefully you are reading this book early in the application cycle. You can acquire a meaningful activity without being involved for years or being elected club president. Volunteer over entire weekends or over the summer to gain substantial hours in a short period. You can also target activities that produce results quickly, such as becoming a Pre-Dental club member and organizing a lecture.

AADSAS does not count activities that you haven't yet started, but it does allow you to describe future planned projects in an activity that you already started. Hence, brainstorm a project to implement or jump onboard an existing project, and start working on it right away.

Application DOs and DON'Ts

Pitfalls to avoid:

- **Not enough dentistry-related experience.** Dental schools are searching for applicants who took the time to truly explore what it means to be a dentist and are sure of their motivations and goals. Yes, it is true that pre-dental applicants have a lot in common with pre-medical and other pre-health applicants. However, if your extracurricular activity profile is heavy on pre-med and includes only fifty hours of total dental experiences, this may be a red flag. In general, aim for 100 hours of shadowing, preferably across different offices and specialties.

- **Overdoing the extracurricular activities.** This may sound counterintuitive, but stuffing too many activities on your application can actually distract from the more impactful ones. There was one applicant several years ago that stood out because the application listed nearly 2,000 hours of research and volunteering across multiple organizations in the three years preceding. What was supposed to dazzle instead became detrimental as the admissions committee debated the likelihood that the applicant exaggerated those numbers and wondered about his or her sociability and integrity. Just because AADSAS allows you to enter in so many activities does not mean you must reach the maximum.

- **Lukewarm letters of recommendation.** Remember the organic chemistry professor you asked for a letter of recommendation?

That letter may not have been as compelling or as unique as you thought. This harkens back to forming robust mentor-mentee relationships and ensuring that you ask for letters from people who truly know you and can speak favorably and specifically about your qualifications and character.

- **Spelling, grammar, and formatting mistakes.** Make sure you dot your i's and cross your t's. Simple errors make you appear hasty, careless, and unprofessional.

- **Not staying organized.** From official transcripts to letters of recommendation to various school-specific requirements, the AADSAS has many moving parts that need to come together for a completed application. We recommend creating a binder or spreadsheet to keep track of these elements, supplemental applications, and deadlines, especially if you tend towards disorganization!

10 General Application Tips

1. **Assess your strengths, weaknesses, and areas of interest before starting the application.** Reflect on what makes you stand out from other applicants (e.g. an unusual college major, unique hobby, research achievement, a hardship you overcame) and areas you want to downplay (e.g. low scores, lack of leadership experience, lack of dental experiences). Use this assessment to ensure your application focuses on the positives as much as possible.

2. **Prepare for the DAT as if it were a separate class.** Even if you already took the classes that cover the DAT test material, you must prepare for the test seriously. Don't start to cram for it two weeks before. Some sections, especially the Perceptual Ability Test and Reading Comprehension, test skills that take time to acquire. It's especially important to get strong DAT scores if you did not do as well in the corresponding basic science prerequisite courses.

3. **Thoroughly research individual schools' requirements.** Some schools have additional requirements for supplemental letters, extra classes, and minimum requirements for dental shadowing and volunteering. A requirement may not be clear-cut (what counts as an upper level mathematics course?). Feel free to email the school's admissions office and explain your situation to check whether you are eligible to apply.

4. **Do not exaggerate or lie.** Every portion of your application is subject to scrutiny and may come up in the interview. Admissions officers sometimes check up on an applicant's credentials. It must be an accurate and fair representation of your academic and extracurricular history. In Section 1, AADSAS asks about incidences of academic dishonesty and probation, and if it applies to you, you must be honest and be prepared to address the incident in the application or interviews.

5. **Review for errors and assess the overall tone.** After you've completed the application, set it aside. Wait for a few days, and reread everything with fresh eyes. Verify the grades you entered and the GPA calculation. Verify the dates of your activities. Ask yourself as if you were an admissions officer: Does this application highlight my strengths and passion for dentistry? How would I describe this applicant? Don't be shy about having a parent, friend, or someone you trust to read the entire package and provide feedback.

6. **Apply as early as you can.** You can submit your application in AADSAS before all the letters of recommendation are submitted, so don't let that hold you up. After you (proudly!) click the submit button, AADSAS may take anywhere from 2-6 weeks to process your application, verify transcripts grades, etc, before forwarding your application onwards. Many schools send application invites on a rolling basis, so you want to be ahead of the pack. Aim to have your application completed by end of July.

7. **Make your supplemental essays specific and well-researched.** Several schools require an additional essay that asks why you are interested in their school. Responses that are simplistic ("School is close to home" or "Because my dad went here") or vague ("Strong academics" or "great reputation") will not help your chances of acceptance. It's a good idea to talk to current students, alumni, and online forums to get a sense of the strengths and weaknesses of each dental school. For more on school research, see Chapters 3 and 4.

8. **Manage your digital and social media presence.** This means ensuring your email username and phone voicemail sound professional, and if needed, creating a new email address. It is a good idea to remove any photos/posts on social media platforms you wouldn't want admissions officers to see and set your accounts on private, at least during the duration of the application cycle.

9. **Monitor the status of your application** periodically over the summer. This includes checking the AADSAS portal and touching base with your letter writers. Don't hesitate to contact the admissions offices with questions or to ensure all pieces of your application have been received.

10. **Relax!** Congratulate yourself on embarking on and finishing this very stressful step. Hopefully you've learned a thing or two about yourself along the way. Dentistry is a very rewarding profession, and this point marks the beginning of your lifelong journey.

Chapter 2

WRITE A WINNING PERSONAL STATEMENT

BY: LILY LIU, DMD AND HELEN YANG, DMD

Most of the dental school application (e.g. your grades, DAT scores, all of your activities and awards) focuses on the past to paint a rough picture of you. Your personal statement, on the other hand, is a blank slate. It is your opportunity to complete the picture of who you are behind the numbers and achievements. When used wisely and strategically, these 4,500 characters can fill gaps in your application, emphasize your desired strengths, and set you apart. This chapter helps you through this process, from designing to writing to editing your own winning personal statement.

What is the purpose of a personal statement?

The website of the American Dental Education Association (the people who run AADSAS) offers this concise answer: "Your personal statement is a one-page essay that gives dental schools a clear picture of who you are and, most importantly, why you want to pursue a career in dentistry." In other words, your essay must answer two key questions: Who are you? and Why dentistry?

To elevate your personal statement, however, your essay should also address the following secondary questions that admissions officers undoubtedly ask themselves:

- What can this applicant contribute to our next class of dental students?

- What can they contribute to the dental profession?

- What can they contribute to the community at large as a student and as a dentist?

- Why does this candidate deserve to be accepted above someone else with similar background, GPA, and test scores?

With that in mind, let's get started! We divided this chapter into (1) brainstorming, (2) writing, and (3) proofreading. The end of the chapter covers pitfalls to avoid and ways to ensure your essay stands out.

Step 1: Let's brainstorm

Everybody has a different approach to writing; there is no right or wrong way. Some people write everything in one marathon session and return to revise later, while others write in segments, revising each paragraph before moving onto the next. Regardless, the importance of brainstorming must not be overlooked. It's difficult to create your masterpiece without first developing a strategic plan.

- **Give yourself plenty of time** to plan, write, and revise. Do not procrastinate and leave it to the last minute. We recommend a minimum of one week because you can set the draft aside and return to it a week later with fresh eyes.

- **Ask a friend/significant other/parent** to help brainstorm. A heartfelt discussion of your strengths and why you're drawn to dentistry can help flesh out your ideas and feelings.

- **Reflect on your "origin" story.** When and how did you decide to become a dentist? Was it through an eureka! moment, or a series of events and circumstances that gradually led you to this realization? The "origin story" is one of the most common themes because it lends itself to answering the two key questions of 'who you are' are 'why dentistry.' Does the idea of being a dentist appeal to you emotionally? Or are you more intellectually drawn to the profession? If you do not think your origin story is particularly exciting or significant to you, there are plenty of other subjects to draw on.

- **Reflect on meaningful experiences**, i.e. moments when you were proud, felt that you made a difference, or encountered a challenge. Think about mentors who inspired you. The experience or mentor need not be related to dentistry or even a medical field (although it could help). Think about what you learned from them, what you learned about yourself, and how they strengthen your resolve to become a dentist. It's important to choose anecdotes colored with vivid details that convey genuine emotion and passion.

- **Survey your strengths, skills,** and other positive personal attributes (a great exercise to prepare for interviews.) Which ones are conducive to becoming a good dentist?

- **Verbalize what you find appealing about the dental profession** and working as a dentist? How do they tie in with the stories you've chosen to tell?
    - **A corollary:** What don't you like about dentistry? It can be helpful to consider aspects about the profession that don't excite you. Is there something you aspire to change within the profession?

- **Arrive at a unifying theme for your essay.** Reading through the winning essays in the second half of this book, you will notice that many of the essays have themes—that is, they're not just random collections of unrelated anecdotes. Each anecdote you chose to include should serve a purpose, and your personal statement should have a theme. How does this theme tie in with the rest of your application?
    - For example, it is perfectly adequate for an essay to state that the applicant derives meaning from helping others (perhaps the most oft cited reason to enter dentistry). One way to improve is elaborate that the applicant loves dentistry because it helps others by putting puzzle pieces together to diagnose the problem and brainstorm different solutions. This would be an effective direction to expand on if the applicant is shown to be a critical thinker and loves intellectual challenges.

- **Consider how your personal statement will complement the rest of your application.** It's a good idea to have worked on the rest of your application before you start writing, so you can objectively survey the whole package. What themes emerge? How would you like to be remembered? You may choose to use the essay to expand on a capstone experience such as organizing an international service trip. Or, you may choose to reveal a side of you that the rest of the application does not show, such as a love for restoring vintage cars or improv comedy. Or, you may use the essay to address perceived weaknesses or fill gaps in the application. For example, if your resume is lacking in leadership positions, you may choose to feature a story of when you demonstrated leadership skills and took initiative.

Step 2: Let's write!

Strong communication skills are essential for all dentists, especially those in positions of leadership in a clinical, academic, or organizational setting. On your way to becoming a dentist, good writing alone may not get you an interview, but bad writing will almost certainly exclude you from one. Of course, everyone writes differently, and different authors choose different stylistic or structural choices with success. Here are a few universal do's and don'ts that apply regardless of your writing style:

- **Show, rather than tell.** Demonstrate instead of merely stating points whenever possible. For example, don't declare that leadership and communication skills are your strengths; prove it through anecdotes. It may be helpful to go through your essay sentence by sentence and ask yourself throughout, "Could I show this more/am I 'telling' too much?"

- **Use active voice.** Use passive voice sparingly and deliberately.

- **Vary sentence and paragraph lengths.** You don't want your essay to sound like a comic book (too many short sentences) or a textbook (too many long sentences). Placing a short, direct sentence after several longer, narrative sentences is especially impactful. It helps to read the sentences aloud to see if they flow together. It works.

- **Let your verbs and nouns do the heavy lifting.** Specific verbs and nouns give a sentence much more weight using less space than do adjectives and adverbs. (e.g. "crept" vs. "walked slowly and quietly"; "masterpiece" vs. "high-level work of art.")

- **Avoid cliches or abstractions.** Be specific.

- **Avoid beginning sentences with "there is" or "there are."** You can almost always rephrase with a more interesting verb than "to be."

- **Don't include lengthy names,** unless necessary. Space is at a premium, and frankly, your readers' eyes will skip past names of long extracurricular titles and organization names. For example, instead of writing "As the Director of Volunteer Outreach and Engagement for the Undergraduate Bioethics Society..." you can state your actions without the long title name. There is also no need to write the exact long names of proteins/gene/bacterial species you researched at the full-name prestigious sounding research institution. Simplify jargon.

- **Don't write really long sentences.** One psychology study found that at 14 words, the average reader could understand more than 90% of the information, but comprehension fell below 10% for a sentence that is 43 words long. Your admissions officer will scan your personal statement and give it three to five minutes at most. Write so your points can be easily and quickly understood. Similarly, don't write really long paragraphs that extend for a third of the entire essay and bury key points in the middle.

There are a number of structural approaches you can take to help unify your essay. A winning essay may include none of the ideas below, but many applicants have used them successfully, so it may be worthwhile to experiment with one or several. Look to the essays in Part II for inspiration.

- **Opening salvo.** Because admissions reps read so many essays, many applicants like to try to open theirs with something attention-grabbing or especially interesting in an attempt to draw in the reader. You may choose to use a first-person narrative, a memorable quotation, an unexpected anecdote, or any other striking opener. If you do decide to do this, it's key that multiple other people read your introduction; the last thing you want to do is shock too much and result in a bad first impression.

- **Chronology.** Many applicants order their essays from childhood to adolescence to adulthood, which is a helpful way to create structure. If you choose this approach, make sure the content is engaging and not too cookie-cutter, especially if you are a more traditional applicant.

- **Reprise.** Humans tend to crave repetition and familiarity; we see this everywhere from pop song choruses to product placement. To use this technique, allude to the opening anecdote or theme later on the essay, or circle back to an opening paragraph at the very end. Beware of sounding gimmicky; don't try to stretch to make things related if they aren't.

- **Before and after.** Growth and redemption are powerful and pervasive themes in popular media, for good reason. To capitalize on this in your essay, tell a story about weakness becoming strength, ignorance becoming wisdom, self-absorption becoming altruism. This can become cheesy, so the challenge is to show nuance and not over-dramatize the before or the after. This structure is good for applicants who already have jobs in non-dental fields.

Step 3: Let's Proofread

Without disciplined proofreading, it's difficult to write a great essay and easy to write a mediocre one. Each of us has a tendency to be in our own heads, and it's this immersive nature of writing that makes proofreading essential. Here are a few keys to successful proofreading:

- **Solicit feedback from your future self.** A major reason to begin working on your essay early is so you will have time to take a few days, or better—a few weeks away from your essay before you submit. After completing your draft, we recommend putting it aside and returning to it at least one week later to read it with fresh perspective as if you were reading someone else's writing for the first time. Be critical. If an anecdote does not have the emotional impact for which you were hoping, reword or remove. We've all had the inclination to cringe at a past piece of writing, and it's this opportunity to cringe that can lead to helpful and needed edits.

- **Proofread again once the rest of the application is finalized.** After you have finalized the rest of your application, reread your essay. Remember, we recommend packaging your entire application, including the essay, with a unifying theme. Add to or trim from your essay to help the overall application's theme feel more cohesive.

- **Proofread as if you're an admissions officer.** If you were reading your own application and had to "sell" yourself, how would you summarize your candidacy in 1-2 sentences? Ask yourself: Is the writer of this essay someone who would excel at this dental school? Is he pleasant and interesting to have as part of the class?

- **Get breadth in your feedback.** Ask both dentists and non-dentists to read your essay. Remember that there's often at least one if not several non-dentists on every admissions committee. Ask people you know well and a few with whom you're less familiar. The former can point out strengths you may have missed and will be more comfortable giving you candid feedback. The latter constitute a better representation of the strangers who will be reading your essay. If a certain point confuses a stranger, most likely it assumes too much, and you need to add more clarifying detail. If you are still in college, many schools have writing centers with employees paid to read or edit student essays—don't be afraid to take advantage of this resource as well.

- **Be specific about the feedback you seek.** Emailing someone your essay and asking "What do you think?" may not yield too many helpful comments. Ask them what parts are interesting or a snooze, what 2-3 adjectives they would use to describe the essay's writer, and other more directed questions. This way, you can shift them closer to the mindset of an admissions committee member.

- **Don't get too attached to words.** If you're having trouble parting with a particular segment of your essay that multiple readers have given a thumbs down, ask yourself: Would you rather have that sentence or an acceptance letter? If a sentence is clunky, re-word. If a paragraph or anecdote lacks the emotional impact you were hoping, re-word or replace. If paragraphs don't quite flow as you hoped, don't hesitate to reorganize.

Pitfalls To Avoid

- **Missing the big picture.** Don't jump right into the writing stage without properly brainstorming and strategizing the best way to frame your essay. Using the first anecdote that jumps to mind, highlighting your longest-participated extracurricular, or using what you think is the most prestigious experience may be okay, but they may not be the best fit for your application strategy.

- **Skipping the final proofread.** Once you click submit in AADSAS, you will be unable to make any changes to the personal statement. Make sure to check the final appearance to edit out misspellings or formatting errors.

- **Too many cooks in the kitchen.** The opposite of the previous pitfall is also a danger. It can be a mistake to over work your essay to satisfy divergent inputs. Too many different people reading your draft and offering suggestions can dilute or drown out your original voice.

- **Grandstanding.** Do not devote an entire paragraph to rattling off achievements, awards, or extracurriculars. We see this commonly in the second half of an essay. It gives the impression that the writer ran out of things to say and is now repeating his or her resume. Not only does this waste precious real estate that could be otherwise better used; it can come across as bragging.

- **Sounding too formal or trite.** A personal statement should be in your authentic, albeit professional, voice. Think about how you would speak during an interview. It helps to read your writing out loud. If there are sentences that sound cliche, insincere, or just too dramatic, it's time to rephrase. Certain words, such as "passionate" and "inspired" tend to get overused in personal statements, so use them sparingly for maximum impact.

- **Telling stories without a takeaway.** Your anecdotes should either explicitly or implicitly discuss their impact on you, what you learned, or how you grew as a person. This is one of the biggest factors that differentiates an excellent essay from an acceptable one. Make sure it is clear what you want the reader to conclude after each anecdote and what personal qualities you seek to highlight. Feedback from other people can help you target paragraphs less effective at achieving this.

- **Plagiarizing.** The story you tell and words you write in your personal statement must be entirely your own. If a reader realizes you pulled from a source without giving proper attribution, your essay will absolutely be dismissed.

- **Specific to one school.** Remember your application will be distributed to every school you apply to. Be careful that your personal statement does not show preference for any specific dental schools.

Making Your Essay Stand Out

Admission directors read hundreds, if not over a thousand, essays each year. To make sure that you're among the select group of applicants invited for an interview, it's not enough to just write a solid essay; yours needs to stand out.

- **Be memorable.** Think about experiences or aspects of your background which few applicants will share. This can be from your upbringing, your hobbies, your interests, or somewhere else. You can also make your essay more memorable via your writing—incorporating a repeating image, phrase, or theme will help it to stick better in a reader's mind, especially if the final image itself is a striking one. Don't be afraid to take a risk here, and if you're worried you've crossed the line from memorable to weird, ask your proofreaders to help you identify if that's the case.

- **Demonstrate maturity.** The average age of a dental school applicant continues to creep up, so especially if you are in college, make sure you have proofreaders who are farther along than you personally and professionally. They can help identify areas where you may come across as less mature. Don't list too many activities, or you'll end up sounding like a high schooler applying for college. A deeper dive into a few impactful experiences allows you to better showcase how you've developed and grown over time. If you are a non-traditional applicant, lean into that, especially if you've had a previous career or have children, to show how you can apply these experiences in your professional life.

- **Demonstrate familiarity with dentistry.** No one expects you to be a dentist already, but showing a nuanced understanding of the profession makes an impression. Learn about the trends and future of the profession, and think about how you specifically will navigate the challenges ahead, as well as what you can add to the profession. Don't be afraid to address the hardships of becoming and being a dentist; no dentist believes that our profession is 100% perfect or easy, and if you write as if that's the case, you'll come across as naive.

The cynical reader might wonder: will applying the suggestions below make your essay too similar to other people's? To that we would say: what make your essay are not these tips and tricks, but **YOU**. We hope that these pointers, as well as the sample essays in the second half of this book, will help you to better think about how to showcase your own unique story.

Chapter 3

ACE THE INTERVIEWS

BY: LAUREN E. KUHN, DMD AND IRINA F. DRAGAN, DDS, MS

Kudos for getting an interview! That means you've passed the toughest round of screenings, and the school is seriously interested in you.

In the past, you may have been encouraged to "Just be yourself!" Unless you're the rare individual who is perpetually well-dressed, well-spoken, and well-informed, we contend that this oft-repeated piece of advice is unhelpful. Instead, we advocate that you become the BEST version of yourself. A successful interview is an intricate, deliberate dance, the culmination of practice, trial and error, and research. Whether this is your first time interviewing or your tenth, read on for our five steps to acing your dental school interview.

Step 1: Self-reflection

Self-reflection is your best friend in preparation. No one knows you like you, and no one is unique in the same way as you. Don't try to become someone you think the admissions officer likes; be your authentic self.

Start with asking yourself some broad, key questions. Think about the type of person you are and how you became the person you are now.

- What sparks your passion?
- If you had to work for free, what job would you choose? Why?
- What are some life-changing experiences you encountered?

- How would your close friends describe you?
- How would your classmates and co-workers describe you?

Reflecting on past experiences allows you to tell vivid and interesting stories. They will have various themes that can be adapted to answer different questions.

- For example, the above story illustrates a defining moment, but it could be used as an answer to "Give an example of a time you were discouraged but persevered" or "Tell us about an experience that shaped you into the person you are today."

Create a list of three to five things that you want the interviewer to remember about you. It can be an accomplishment that you are proud of, an unique hobby or talent, or a particularly compelling reason you wish to pursue dentistry. These facts and anecdotes should be selected to highlight and strengthen your narrative and make you seem like an interesting and outstanding person. Practice weaving them into your answers. The following are examples:

- "As a child, I was nervous about dental appointments. I remember feeling sick to my stomach before appointments and crying before, during, and after my visits. I've always found it rewarding to work with people who are nervous or apprehensive, because it is an opportunity to put them at ease and show that I care. When I shadowed Dr. Joe last year, I saw how his kindness and ability to explain procedures made appointments more predictable for patients and helped them feel comfortable."

- "I'd like to tell a story about responding to a medical emergency on an airplane and what steps I took to stay calm in this situation. I think this story can help the interviewer understand my willingness to help others and ability to handle urgent challenges."

- "My prosthodontist in college had a significant influence on me. Going through the long process of getting two implants gave me the patient's perspective and taught me a lot about being a good doctor."

- "I held four jobs during college and to maximize my time, I audio recorded my notes from class. This enabled me to effectively balance studying with my other obligations. I am good at handling a busy schedule."

- "I love teaching and explaining things to people, and I love the challenges of finding different ways to present the same information until it clicks for my students. I understand there is a need for more dental educators, and I definitely see teaching, either part time at dental school or at a clinic externship, playing a significant role in my career.

Step 2: Let's Practice

With a good sense of what you have to offer and what stories you want to share, now you can prepare a list of potential interview questions. Look for examples on websites and in books. Try to anticipate questions the interviewer might ask after reading your application.

Now, write mock questions onto small slips of paper, place them in a bowl or on flashcards, draw questions at random and practice answering them out loud. Make a goal for how many questions you will practice each night. If you're preparing several weeks in advance, perhaps practice three questions per day. If your interview is in a couple days, you may want to practice 5-10 questions each night.

Remember: this is not an exercise in memorizing future answers. Rather, it is to prime your brain to think quickly, speak clearly, and allow your words to describe the person you are, emphasizing examples from your past and your plans for the future. You can start by practicing alone. Then, start practicing your answers in front of a mirror. After a few sessions, try video recording yourself and critiquing the content of your answers, the smoothness of your delivery, and your body language.

Here are some commonly asked interview questions:

A. Questions about your background

- Tell me about yourself (most interviews seem to start this way.)

- How do you spend your time when not studying?
- What was your favorite extracurricular activity and why? What did you learn from it?
- (If you are transitioning careers) What inspired you to change careers? How can your first career help you become a better dentist?
- Describe an ethical dilemma you faced and how you handled it.

B. Why dentistry?

- Why do you want to pursue dentistry?
- What have you learned from shadowing dentists?
- What do you think is the biggest issue that dentistry faces?
- Where do you see yourself in ten years?

C. Why this school?

- Why do you want to attend our school?
- What are you looking for in a dental school?
- What do you think you can contribute to your dental school class?
- What can you contribute to the field of dentistry? How does it support our school's mission and vision?

D. Interpersonal skills

- What is your greatest strength? Weakness?
- Give us an example when you led your team successfully and one example when you could have led differently. What would you improve from the last example?
- How do you deal with conflict?
- What kind of leader are you?

Now, here are some questions to help you critique your own responses:

- Are my answers too long? Am I rambling and monologuing instead of making the interview more of a conversation?
- Am I using "ummm," "like," or other common fillers?

- Am I too vague? Do I make statements without giving concrete examples?
- What does my body language convey? Confidence or arrogance? Disinterest? Nervousness?

After critiquing your private video interviews, you are ready for a mock interview. We recommend at least two practice interviews, but you should use your discretion to decide what is best for you. It can be with colleagues, family, friends, advisors, or your school's career center. A combination of opinions from mock interviewers can help you feel more prepared.

When soliciting feedback, many of your mock interviewers may default to giving vague responses such as "You did a good job." It's up to you to ask for targeted feedback, especially about questions for which you felt unprepared. For example:

- Did I look surprised or caught off guard during such-and-such a question?
- Did I start answering too quickly?
- Did I come across as too rehearsed?
- Did you find the anecdote about so-and-so boring?
- If you had to summarize our interview, which responses or anecdotes impressed you favorably?

Step 3: Look Like a Future Dentist

Dressing for success will start your interview day on the right track. Interviewers meet many candidates, and the first impression sets the tone of the interaction between candidate and evaluator. It does not mean you must wear a prescribed ensemble. When you love what you are wearing, you're more likely to feel true to yourself and convey excitement and confidence during the interview. Consider the following:

- Your attire should be clean (no pet hair, lint, stains, or wrinkles.)

- Your clothing should be well tailored. Poorly-fitting clothing, such as pants that are too short, can be perceived as a lack of preparedness or lack of attention to detail.
- Is your outfit too loose or too tight?
- Are your shoes or accessories (briefcase, purse) scuffed or in poor shape?
- (For women) Is your shirt buttoned to an appropriate level?

Here are some ways to look memorable yet professional:

- Royal blue or navy blue suits and dresses can help you stand out in a sea of black and gray suits.
- Different tailoring or structure of your attire can help you show your style. For ladies, a mandarin collar, ¾ length jacket, or understated belt might add the uniqueness you're looking for. For men, wear a suit jacket in blue, gray, or black with two buttons. Tailoring may help you feel more confident in your business attire.
- Classic jewelry (pearls, gold, silver, etc.), and other tasteful accessories can complete an outfit that will help you appear more polished.

Ladies: Understated makeup (i.e. mascara, lipstick) is appropriate, as long as it gives a professional and natural appearance. Many applicants have been told by their advisors or family to wear no makeup; however it is acceptable and even recommended if it makes you feel more confident, authentic, and professional. Hair should be away from the face and eyes. Fingernails should be natural or coated in fresh, smooth polish. Close-toed heels are appropriate, but it may be a good idea to also pack flats; most interviews include a school tour.

Men: Hair should appear well-groomed and orderly. Mild use of hair gel or products is acceptable. Facial hair should appear well-maintained. Ties and socks can be of bold colors as long as they are not distracting.

Step 4: The Interview

Take a few deep breaths. You are ready for this. This is a chance for the interviewer to get to know you beyond the AADSAS, so let your personality show. Your interviewer will most likely be either faculty or an upper-level dental student. Most interviews are one-on-one and last 30 to 45 minutes.

Throughout the interview, your interviewer will expect you to ask them questions. Try to ask questions that show you've done your research and are familiar with the school. Avoid asking questions that can be easily searched online.

Questions to learn more facts about the school:

- Does the school teach usage of recent technologies, such as CEREC and digital dentistry?
- What kind of implant training do dental students receive?
- Does the school offer research funding?
- When do students start seeing patients in clinic? Are students responsible for finding their own patients?
- What opportunities does the school offer for students who are interested in specializing?
- What is the school policy on participating in outside activities and organizations, such as ASDA or SNDA?

Open-ended, opinion questions for the interviewer:

- Can you describe the academic culture here?
- What kind of relationships do students have with the professors and administration?
- How active are student groups on campus?
- What is one thing you would change about this school?

Some of your interviewers may not have had a chance to read your application prior to meeting you. You should arrive with a few copies of the following:

- **Resume.** Remember to keep it concise, ideally one page. You can ask your interviewer if he or she wishes to have a copy at the beginning.
- **Personal statement**
- **Photos** to support your activities and hobbies, if applicable. One of the authors of this book is an origami enthusiast (which helped with the manual dexterity question) and brought photos of some elaborate projects. If the conversation landed on this topic she brought the photos out to show.

The interview is longer than you think:

Assume it starts the moment you arrive on campus and ends when you arrive home. The staff do pay attention to candidates' interactions with each other and staff. They notice which candidates exhibit certain characteristics, such as being shy, attentive, overpowering, or outgoing. They notice when people are texting, appear distracted, or seem unjustifiably confident. Even though these individuals may not be official interviewers, they can report their observations to the admissions committee. The opinion of a non-voting member—such as a student you ate lunch with or an interview coordinator—can actually sway the vote. This has been shown to be true through discussions with admissions officers and also the personal experience of the authors.

Some schools will organize night socials or arrange for you to stay with a current student. Be on your best behavior. You can be sure that any wayward, rude, or strange behavior (getting inebriated at the social, pestering your host with too many questions) will be noted, and word will spread to the admissions committee. Again, consider yourself to be in interview mode and be friendly with everyone from the security guard to your fellow interviewees as soon as you arrive.

Step 5: Follow Up

Now that the interview is behind you, don't forget these post-interview action-points:

- **Send or email thank you notes** to interviewers and one to the admissions staff as a whole. This is a must!! You would be surprised by how many interviewees forget this critical step or neglect to write down the name and email of their interviewers. Mention specifics about what you enjoyed about the interview day and your experience at the school. Did you appreciate that the admissions staff arranged for dental students to have lunch with you? Did you enjoy your conversation about oral surgery with your first interviewer of the day? Let her know!

- This should be done within 3 days of the interview, before the interviewer has completed their post-interview report.

- **Send a quick update to the schools** if you have major changes to your qualifications during the period between your interview and the time when the school announces its admissions decisions. Here are some examples:

  - You received a 4.0 for your Fall semester and made Dean's List. Send an updated transcript and a note letting the admissions staff know that you appreciate the time they are taking to review your new and improved transcript.

  - You've been informed that your research paper was accepted for publication.

Frequently Asked Questions:

Q) How do I approach answering "Tell me about yourself."

This is the one question for which we recommend having a prepared concise response. You want to appear personable and interesting. Consider the picture you want to paint for the interviewer and what facts you wish to highlight at the beginning. For example, if the theme to emphasize is one of success in spite of struggles, start by explaining your past. It is smart to end your response on an interesting topic that sets you up for some follow-up questions. Here is an example:

"My name is Jane, and I'm from New York City. When I was three years old, my family immigrated to the United States from Poland. I grew up with a loving family. As I grew up, I realized my English skills were not as strong as others, since we didn't speak it at home. I also did not understand all of the available after school activities or resources available to me. Because of my upbringing, I am someone who recognizes the struggles for working parents and immigrant families. I also appreciate that I had to work harder than many of my peers to receive high marks in English and writing, and I'm grateful to my parents that they nurtured and helped me remain fluent in Polish. My background is what helped me become the resilient person I am today..."

Q) How do I respond if I don't know the answer to a question?

- Let the interviewer know you're not familiar with the topic, but make an educated guess and pivot to a topic you do know.
    - For example, if you were asked "What do you think is the biggest challenge facing the field of dentistry today?" Perhaps you don't feel you have a perspective on the field globally or on a large-scale. You can draw off the experiences you do have. You could say: "I don't feel I can speak to the state of dentistry on a large-scale, however, when I was shadowing Dr. Smith in my hometown, I noticed that one of the biggest challenges was finding affordable treatment options for patients. It is my hope that in the future we will find a way to help patients afford the care they need."

- Ask the interviewer for their insight into the topic.
    - For example, if you were asked "What do you think is the impact of Dental Service Organizations on dentistry?" You may respond: "I'm not familiar with DSOs. Can you clarify what they are?" or "If you have any insight you would like to share, I'd appreciate your perspective on it."

- End by saying you are curious about the topic.
    - For example, if you were asked, "What do you know about dental mid-level providers?" You may respond: "I'm not

familiar with this topic, but our discussion piqued my interest and I'm going to look into this."

Q) How can I show my top choice school that I really want to go there?

- **Show the school's culture and core values align with your vision and goals.** For example, some schools are known for emphasizing research and academia, others for producing stronger clinicians. What you chose to highlight during the interview should present a solid case that you fit right in.

- **Show familiarity with the school.** From the types of questions you ask to the casual conversation, you want to show that you have done your research. During your interview prep, ask around to connect with students and alumni of the school, and respectfully ask if they are willing to share information and opinions.

- **Keep in touch with the school.** Many of the schools have "Pre-Dental Day" events; find out if the schools you are interested in are hosting any of them. If they do, try to arrange the schedule to attend. It will give you an overview of the program, and will certainly help relieve stress on the actual interview day. If you return to a place you've been already, you will certainly feel more comfortable. In addition, some of the staff members might remember you when the big interview day comes.
  - ADEA organizes an online Virtual Fair for pre-dental students, where admissions officers and dental students answer questions. Find out more personal information about particular schools there, and bring them up during your interview process.

- **Finally, do not be shy.** Be straightforward and sincerely acknowledge that this is your top school, preferably near the end of the interview, in your closing statement. It is impactful if you say this AFTER you have done the previous steps and shown that you are a great fit.

Q) Does it hurt or help to declare an interest in a particular specialty?

If you have a very strong interest or curiosity for one or two specialties, it does not hurt to mention it. Many applicants express interest in the popular specialties such as oral surgery or orthodontics, so your experiences should back up your interest, such as via significant research or mentors in that field or exposure to that field as a patient. Keep in mind, however, that a dental school's aim is to first produce competent general dentists, so you must avoid giving the impression you are not open to learning general dentistry.

A few schools have a reputation for sending large numbers of their graduates onto specialty residencies, while others are known for having strong broad, general dentistry curricula. It's wise to know this about the school in advance.

Q) What do I do if the interview is awkward and not going well?

Much like if you were on a date, you should pay close attention to your interviewer's behavior, feelings, and body language. Ideally, they will appear engaged and interested in what you have to say, but if you feel that is not the case, try these suggestions to change the mood:

- **Check that you are not monologuing.** The interview should be a conversation that flows between topics and questions. If you notice yourself talking for too long or telling a very long story, pause. Give your interviewer a chance to respond, or ask a different question.

- **Pivot to a new topic.** Perhaps you talked about your research or job for several minutes now, and you notice the interviewer's eyes are wandering. You should swiftly wrap up that topic and introduce a new one. For example, you can say "The zebrafish project is ongoing and I hope to publish my results within a year or two. Lately, I've been learning more about the important access to care issues in dentistry, and I have been brainstorming potential projects that I can do in dental school to address this question."

- **Ask your interviewer a question.** Most people like to hear themselves talk. If you shine the spotlight onto your interviewer by asking a series of intelligent questions, listening attentively, that can change the tone of the interview. To continue the example above, you can ask "...what kind of research projects have you or your peers done in dental school? Is there anyone doing research on access to care?... That sounds really interesting, what's the name of that faculty member? I'd love to contact them."

Q) What's the best way to wrap up an interview?

You should know how long the interview is, and try to steer it to a purposeful conclusion, rather than it ending abruptly by running out of things to talk about or running out of time. With five minutes left, think about whether you covered the three to five main points you intended to cover. Prepare a 30-second conclusion that reiterates your desire to attend this school and why you are a great fit, and thank the interviewer for wonderful conversation and for sharing their opinions of the school with you.

Q) What role does the interview actually play in the admissions process?

The purpose of the interview is to put a face to an application that has already been deemed acceptable. It's a critical piece of the application puzzle for the school to get a sense of what kind of role you can fulfill at the dental school. It's okay to be a little nervous, but don't forget to let your personality shine through.

At minimum, the interview must establish that you are a pleasant person to spend time with, that you can carry a conversation, that you can be professional, and that you are a critical thinker, especially when faced with a question on topics you're not familiar with. Red flags include the converse of the aforementioned points, and you can be sure they are brought up during committee deliberations. Examples include too many awkward silences, overtly competitive or rude behavior when mingling with other interviewees, appearing disinterested or unknowledgeable about the school, and inability to articulate why you want to do dentistry or answer basic questions, such as about hobbies.

TOP 10 Tips to Rock Your Interview

1. Research the school online and remember key facts about the school and details that appeal to you.

2. After doing some serious introspection, prepare three to five key facts or stories about yourself to make sure to discuss in every interview. These can be unique facts about yourself, impressive accomplishments, or something very specific to this school that appeals to you, etc.

3. Practice interview questions alone at first. Practice aloud, then in a mirror, then video record yourself. Critique and repeat.

4. Do practice mock interviews.

5. Be on time. This means arrive 10-15 minutes early.

6. Interact and engage in friendly conversation with everyone you come across on interview day. That includes support staff, current students, other candidates, etc.

7. Steer the interview to a purposeful conclusion. Avoid finishing with the interviewer saying "Okay, our time is up." Instead, be proactive, make sure you have covered your main points (see bullet #2), and ask if there is anything else you can answer to help them make a decision.

8. Send a thank you note to all of your interviewers, and send important updates/ new achievements you think the admissions committee should know.

9. Don't forget that while the school is evaluating you, you are also evaluating the school! The interview is your chance to critically appraise the school's strengths and weaknesses, so don't be afraid to ask some tough questions (preferably to people not involved in admissions), and decide if you really want to spend four years there.

10. In spite of the interview jiggers, try to have fun! Many friendships are started on the interview trail, so enjoy this experience.

Chapter 4

MAP YOUR ROAD
TO DENTAL SCHOOL

BY: HELEN YANG, DMD AND SANGITA MURALI, MS

While the first three chapters examined the application cycle in depth, this chapter looks at the big picture: how to best prepare in the years and months leading up to the application, what to look for when picking schools, and what to do after it's over (if you can imagine that far ahead). The common theme is: the earlier you start planning, the more prepared you'll be when application season arrives.

General Pre-Dental Application Cycle Timeline

2+ years before:

- **Academics:**
  - **Plan your coursework** to be on track to complete all the prerequisite courses.
    - Dental schools look favorably upon elective courses in the social sciences and business such as sociology, psychology, and accounting.
  - **Keep your grades as high as possible,** especially science classes. Aim for a GPA of at least 3.6, the national average GPA of admitted dental students. If you wish to apply for competitive schools, aim for a GPA of 3.8+.

- **Develop good study habits** and learn to prepare for exams. This is especially important for those who tend to rely on their natural smarts to breeze through college classes. Dental school expects you to learn massive amounts of information in a short time, and the ones who struggle in classes often failed to develop good study habits and budgeted their time poorly.

- **Extracurricular activities:**

  - **Get involved in a broad range of activities** that represent your interests, from student groups to volunteering to hobbies. See chapter 1 for more on extracurriculars.

  - **Explore research,** if interested. It usually takes at least one year to achieve tangible research results.

  - **Shadow at dental offices.** At the beginning, it's a good idea to rotate through several offices for only 1-2 days each.

- **Personal life:**

  - **Reflect on your strengths and weaknesses** and consider how you can better prepare to become a dentist. This includes strengthening skills such as manual dexterity.

  - **Explore different careers** to ensure dentistry is the one for you.

  - **Start saving for dental school.** Maintain good credit scores to help obtain private loans with better interest rates later.

1 year before (For traditional applicants, this is junior year of college):

- **Academics:**

  - **Maintain a high GPA.** If your science GPA is not as strong, consider taking additional science courses.
  - **Be familiar with the DAT** subjects and exam format. There are Facebook groups and email lists you can join to receive free daily DAT prep tips.

- **Extracurricular activities:**

- **Draft a resume.** Think about what is lacking (for example, too few volunteer hours or no significant leadership positions). Apply for leadership opportunities when they arise.
  - Try to have two activities that you remain involved with for longer than one year.
- **Continue to shadow various general dentists and specialists.** Start thinking about who you want to ask for a letter of recommendation, and arrange to spend more time with that particular dentist.
- If possible, **attend a dental conference** or events at nearby dental schools. You will meet other pre-dental and current dental students and gain valuable insights into the profession. One good conference is the ASDA National Leadership Conference, held every fall in Chicago.

6 months before:

- **Academics:**
  - **Draft a list of potential mentors** from whom you can request letters of recommendation. Maintain relationships with them through periodic check-ins.
  - **Start actively preparing for the DAT exam.** Treat it like an additional class commitment and scale back on extracurricular activities during that semester.
    - Pre-dents on average spend 300-500 hours preparing for the exam. Some people prefer to spread out studying over several months, while others prefer a few weeks of concentrated studying. Find what works for you.
  - **Register for a DAT test date.**
    - After your test application is approved and you received an ADA DENTPIN, you have six months to take the exam. Most pre-dents take the DAT for the first time between November and May before the application

cycle. This leaves the possibility to retake the exam should you be dissatisfied with your score.

- When you register, we recommend sending your scores to EVERY dental school where you think you might apply. Most schools will not look at the score unless they receive a completed AADSAS application. These initial score reports are free, but adding additional schools later incurs additional fees.

- **Extracurricular Activities:**

  - **Review your activities and achievements.** There is still enough time to achieve tangible, impressive results.

  - If you have been doing research, consider **presenting a poster at a conference** or giving an oral presentation to your department.

- **Other:**

  - **Research and create a preliminary list of dental schools.** Visit campuses, and contact current students to learn more about the schools and the cities in which they are located. Online discussion forums such as Student Doctor Network are a treasure trove of information.

One month before:

- **Retake the DAT** if needed.

- **Continue to stay involved with your extracurriculars.**

- **Finalize your list of schools.** According to an ADEA survey, pre-dental students on average apply to nine to ten schools.

  - If your application is not very competitive or if you are an international applicant, consider adding more schools to your list, especially ones with large entering classes (such as New York University, Tufts University, Boston University, Temple University). It is not unusual to apply to upwards of 15 schools.

- **Start your application:**
  - Draft your personal statement.
  - Request transcripts from every school you've received course credit, including summer or study abroad schools.
  - Update your resume.
  - Request new or updated letters from mentors.
  - If eligible, assemble paperwork to qualify for the AADSAS Fee Assistance Program.
  - Find people to conduct mock interviews with you.
- **Create an application budget.** Applicants typically spend several thousand dollars during an application cycle. Costs include:
  - DAT fees:
    - Registration. At the time of writing, registration costs $415.
    - Test preparation materials
    - Fee to send additional score reports, if needed
  - AADSAS fees:
    - The fee for the first school is currently $245, and $99 for each additional school.
    - Some schools have secondary application fees ranging from $50 to $100.
  - University transcript fees
  - Interview costs (Transportation, lodging, incidentals, interview attire)

Choosing the right school for you:

We compiled a list of the many factors that can impact your dental school experience. Consider which ones are important vs must-have when creating your initial list of schools and making a final choice between several programs.

Location:

- Urban vs suburban vs. rural. Can you see yourself living in that area for four years?

- How far are you willing to be from your family/partner/close friends?

- If you wish to attend an out-of-state school and intend to return home to practice, ask if your school supports the necessary licensure boards exams required by your state.

Cost of attendance:

- Total cost of attendance includes:
    - Tuition (typically increases by 3-5% from year to year)
    - Supplemental fees (e.g. clinic fees, equipment, books, health insurance, university fees)
    - Cost of living (e.g. room and board, transportation, miscellaneous)

- Remember to factor in interests owed on loans (most people pay back their school loans between 10-15 years).

Academics:

- Some programs use a "pass/fail" system, while others give letter grades. Both types of schools have similar success with their students passing the national board examinations and being accepted into residency programs. Anecdotally, students have reported that a P/F curriculum is less stressful.

- Does the school offer opportunities to obtain additional degrees such as MS, MPH, MBA, or PhD?

Clinical training:

- Find out when dental students begin treating patients and what clinical opportunities first year students have.

- Learn about the transition from pre-clinical to clinical years and if the school has in place "big brothers and sisters" mentoring program to share tips and practical knowledge.

- Ask how much exposure students get to modern technologies such as CAD/CAM, digital dentistry, cosmetic dentistry, implant surgical and restorative training.

- Learn about community-based health initiatives and service-learning opportunities at your dental school and in the surrounding areas.

Extracurriculars

- Does the school support students' involvement in organized dentistry? Many dental students point to being involved in ASDA, SNDA, ADEA, or dental fraternities as a highlight of their dental school experience. These groups offer leadership positions on local, state, and national levels, as well as opportunities to meet fellow students and dentists from around the country.

- Does the school encourage and support students to engage in research? Inquire about grants or scholarships offered for dental students. Some schools offer funding to cover costs associated with traveling to major conferences such as AADR and ADEA meetings to present research.

Post-graduation

- Learn about a school's graduation rate and how many students complete their clinical requirements on time. Many residency programs begin in July and even as early as June so planning ahead is critical to ensure you will make it to your post-graduate program on time.

- If you are considering specializing, find out how recent graduates fared in their applications and where they ended up. Ask current students about the level of mentorship they receive from specialist faculty members.

- Learn about the resources offered by the school to help apply for jobs.

The overall "vibe."

- Observe how students interact with each other and with faculty. Is the environment intense? If so, do you enjoy that? Do current students report really high levels of stress? Do they look happy?
- Do you have a positive impression of the community? Choosing a culture that suits your personality and where you feel at home is critical to help you through the highs and lows of dental school.

What's next?

If you have been accepted by one or more dental schools:

CONGRATULATIONS!! We remember very well the exultation of receiving those happy emails and phone calls. Be proud that your hard work has come to fruition, and get excited for a new phase of life.

- **Update your mentors** after you're accepted into a program expressing your appreciation for taking you under their wings. These people went to great lengths to help shape your success and will share in your joy.

- **Finish all your classes and requirements on a strong note,** if applicable.

- **How to spend the summer before 1st year?** Many people choose to spend that summer working to save money. While that is admirable, we do recommend taking several weeks to relax and recharge. That Europe trip or Yellowstone camping trip you've been dreaming about? Now is the time to do it! Dental school, especially the first two years, is rigorous, and there won't be an opportunity to take extended breaks once it begins.

- **Research how to finance your dental school education.** Since the bulk of financial aid (and all federal aid programs) are loans rather than scholarships, be prepared to borrow. Your school's

Financial Aid office should be your go-to resource to understand all of your options.

- **Institutional programs.** Grants and scholarships awarded directly from the university may include merit-based, need-based, and endowed scholarship funds. Unfortunately, most schools do not offer significant scholarships.

- **Federal student aid.** Federal loans offer some advantages over private loans, including fixed interest rates, ability to defer or enter forbearance, and different options for repayment.

- **Private loans.** Interest is based entirely on your or your co-signer's credit scores and tend to vary over the life of the loan. You may not have the ability to defer payments should you enter residency or are in between jobs.

- **Private scholarships** by companies, dental organizations, non-profit organizations.

- **Return of service programs**
  - Health Professions Scholarship Program (HPSP). For US citizens only. If selected, this program covers 100% of tuition, fees, and living costs and provides a stipend. For each year in the program, you are expected to serve on active duty for the same number of years. Visit the Air Force, Army, and Navy websites for more information.
  - National Health Service Corps Scholarship (NHSC). If selected, it covers 100% of your tuition and fees, and provides a modest monthly living stipend. After graduation, you are expected to work in clinics in medically underserved community and/or rural areas.

The waitlist.

Given how competitive the application process is, many wonderful and highly qualified applicants are placed on waitlists each year. If this happens to you, don't despair— you are still in the running! Remember that the acceptance timeline is several months long. You must stand out and ensure that you are on the school's radar should new spots become available.

- **Thank the admissions officers** for their time, and state explicitly that dentistry is your dream career and that their program is your top choice.

- **Update them on new accomplishments.** Send an email informing them of awards you've received, research progress, and other activities related to dentistry since your interview. This is to show admissions officers that you are not only passionate about the field but are continuously immersed in learning and achieving more.

- **Reiterate your strong interest in this program**, and this time, be really specific. Give examples and anecdotes from the school tour and interview, and make the case that you are best equipped to take advantage of the school's resources.

- **Arrange to visit the school again** and talk to the admissions officers, if possible. Politely ask what you can do to improve the chances of receiving an offer.

If you were not accepted to a dental school this cycle:

Many dental students have applied two to three times before successfully matriculating. Even if you don't get in this year, you can still cultivate good relationships with your top schools' admissions officers so that they can reconsider you more seriously next year. Here are a few steps you can take to become a more competitive applicant in the next cycle:

- **Identify weaknesses in your application.** This requires serious self-reflection and heartfelt conversations with people you trust.
  - Ask yourself if one section of your DAT is much lower than others. Did you apply late in the cycle? Did you apply to too few schools? How did your interviews go? What kind of first impression do you make? When you apply again, you must show how you've become a

stronger applicant, whether it means retaking the DAT, applying earlier next cycle, improving your science GPA, or practicing maintaining composure even with tough interview questions.

- You can email admissions officers to ask politely if there were red flags in your application that precluded you from consideration. Chances are, you won't receive a straightforward answer, but in rare cases someone may point you in the right direction.

- **Stay in touch with your mentors,** and reinforce that you intend to apply again. If you choose to rely on the same mentor next year, they should update their letter rather than reuse the identical old letter.

- **Address low GPA.** If your undergraduate GPA is not competitive, consider taking post-baccalaureate classes, especially in the science, to raise your GPA. Another good option is to pursue a master's program, such as a MPH or MS, to show admissions you can handle a rigorous academic curriculum.

- **Solidify post-grad plans that immerse yourself in dentistry,** even better if that position allows you access to your top choice school's community. If research is your thing, apply to be a technician at a dental school's research lab. Consider dental assisting for a year to learn more about the profession and day-to-day tasks. This will show admissions' officers that you are passionate and truly motivated.

We hope the pearls of wisdom in this chapter have broken down what can feel like an overwhelming process into more manageable steps. Best of luck, and look to the next section of successful essays for more inspiration!

PART II

1. AMY'S ESSAY

I will never forget the big, toothy grin from an elderly lady during my first dental shadowing experience. She had just received new dentures, and she was so thrilled about being able to speak and chew normally again that she couldn't stop smiling. Speaking, chewing, smiling; I'd always taken these simple abilities for granted. That changed during my senior year of high school when I set up a shadowing opportunity with Dr. M, a local dentist. As I observed Dr. M complete restorations, extract teeth, and fabricate dentures for his patients, I began to consider pursuing dentistry as a career. I was touched by how a seemingly small dental procedure made such a huge difference in someone's life.

I entered college with plans to pursue dentistry, but I explored other fields as well, to expand my horizons. Early on in my college career, I became fascinated with neuroscience, drawn by how it connects physiology to behavior. Eager to get my hands wet, I worked as both a clinical monitor in a sleep lab and as a technician in a neurology basic research lab.

The sleep lab ran fourteen day inpatient studies about the effects of sleep deprivation on healthy adults. The battery of cognitive tests and chronic sleep deprivation often left the subjects drained so I tried different ways to make their experience more bearable. When there was downtime in the study protocol, I chatted with the subjects, played Monopoly with them, and even braided one woman's hair. I felt satisfied knowing that my simple actions made someone else's day better, and I became connected to each person that I worked with during the studies. My experiences as a clinical monitor confirmed that

I want a career that gives me the chance to make a difference in the well-being of others.

The basic research lab that I worked in uses the nematode *C. elegans* as a neurological model. In addition to pouring agar plates and mixing reagents for work study, I also conducted an independent research project to study the expression and function of a class of genes encoding prion-like proteins in *C. elegans*. One of the methods that I used was DNA transformation via microinjection, which involved synthesizing reporter DNA using PCR, injecting it into the gonads of adult wild-type worms, and observing the transformed progeny under a fluorescent microscope. During the process of conducting experiments, I realized that I loved working with my hands. Performing manual tasks such as transferring worms under a microscope with a metal pick and injecting DNA into microscopic worm gonads came easily to me. I even found these tasks therapeutic; time passed quickly while I conducted my experiments. Because of my lab experiences, I feel more prepared and confident in my ability to learn the difficult manual skills of dentistry.

Outside of research, one of my greatest passions is dance. The Pan-Asian Dance Troupe was the first "club" I joined in college, although it's really more of a family. Through dance, I've gained a new understanding of the power of teamwork. A simple arm movement can become magnificent when performed in synchronization with a large group. As artistic director, I became responsible for coordinating practices and overseeing the production of our annual show. Finding practice space and scheduling over a dozen dances weekly to fit the schedules of busy troupe members was no easy task. It required a great deal of organization and consistent communication with the entire troupe. Being in a dance troupe has taught me more than how to move gracefully to music, it has taught me how to be a team player and a leader.

Ultimately, the culmination of my college experiences have confirmed my desire to pursue dentistry. I seek a happy medium between my two research experiences; I crave both the social interactions of being a clinical monitor well as the intellectual and technical challenges of conducting independent *C. elegans* research.

Furthermore, I seek a career where I can work on a team with other professionals and have opportunities for leadership. Being a dentist would allow me to feel fulfillment through helping others, satisfy my curiosity for science, and provide an outlet for me to work with my hands. I am pursuing dentistry because I want my career to be more than just a profession; I want it to also be my passion. Someday, I hope to help others speak, chew, and smile, just like Dr. M.

* * *

Commentary:

This is one of the rare essays that describes how she came to the conclusion to pursue dentistry intellectually without relying too much on the common "I hurt my tooth" or "I want to help people" narratives. She likes working with people and goes above and beyond with her sleep medicine cognitive testing studies to relate to patients and pick up on cultural nuances. I enjoyed the deft way she integrated her research experiences into the essay and thought the awareness she has about how manual dexterity skills required of a scientist translates to dentistry was notable. The author highlights the importance of teamwork through her experiences as an artistic director and understands how being organized and an approachable leader will serve her well lifelong!
—*Sangita Murali*

Author Bio:
- Amy Yu
- University of Pennsylvania, Neurobiology, Class of 2016
- Harvard School of Dental Medicine, Class of 2020
- "I knew I wanted to pursue a career in dentistry since the beginning of college and went straight through to dental school. I chose to major in Neurobiology because it's fascinating and because it fulfilled most of my pre-dental requirements. Outside of school, I was the artistic director of an Asian cultural dance troupe and danced in a modern dance company. Additionally, I love to cook and was the culinary director of a food magazine on campus. Finally, I worked and conducted research in a basic science lab, and I wrote my senior thesis on a class of prion-like proteins *in C. elegans*."

2. ANDREW'S ESSAY

I was ten when I had my first tooth pulled. I was shocked when my dentist told me that it was going to be an adult upper right lateral incisor in the front of my mouth. There was a time when my friends and I would have been proud to display the space left behind after losing our primary teeth; it was a rite of sorts into "adulthood." Yet this was different—this was permanent: there was going to be no glory from this loss. Each time I saw my incomplete smile after the extraction, I became increasingly self-conscious of my malocclusion. Because of this, one of the most exciting days of my life was the day I got braces. As the orthodontic treatment progressed, I slowly began to regain the self-confidence I had lost because of the extraction. It now seems trivial that so much of my pre-teen identity was tied to a gap in my teeth. Yet it is because I was able to regain an aesthetically pleasing smile through the work of my orthodontist that I find so much value in the impact of dentistry upon a patient.

To this day, what amazes me most about my orthodontist is his artistic skill. Watching him expertly bend my archwires was mesmerizing; he seemed to know how to kink the wire to move my teeth millimeters into the ideal position. This aspect of dentistry—the artistic side—is what I find so interesting and unique. It is a career in which I can help patients achieve, regain, or preserve oral function in practical ways, while at the same time combining aesthetics and artistry. I realized how compelling this was while walking away from my first drill and fill lab with our dental science club. The thirty minutes I spent packing and smoothing amalgam into my drilled tooth felt very much like an art project; smoothing the shiny metal along the curves and crevices of the tooth was like shaping and molding clay. Yet this was more than a simple sculpture lesson—this was a treatment for real patients experiencing real pain. I found that I could enjoy the attention to detail and the artistry of the procedure while providing potentially life-changing care.

Perhaps the most significant aspect of dentistry for me is the interpersonal care that is extended to the patient. In the months after my extraction, each dentist that I visited showed me that they cared about more than my teeth: they cared about my well-being as an individual. They were tremendously patient, answering my nitpicky questions and slowly but surely giving me assurance that I could trust their work. It is in college that I have realized the challenges and joys of gaining the trust of others. As a part of Asian InterVarsity, a Christian organization dedicated to evangelism and outreach, I have spent many hours meeting with students. Often strangers, these classmates initially have no reason to trust me. Yet to facilitate deeper and more intimate conversation, I have explored ways to connect with them. Time after time, I find that this link, anything from a shared experience to a similar sense of humor, is the spark in developing significant, trusting relationships. Such interactions were the crux of my own experiences with the dentists who helped me overcome my fear of smiling; my relational trust in them and their work prompted me to pursue the treatment that has given me such a unique smile. The same trust building motivates me to provide equally transforming experiences through dental care—the impression that I can have upon these individual's lives makes the uncertainty of reaching beyond my relational comfort zone worth it.

Looking at the peers and professionals I have met during my undergraduate career, it has become more evident to me that the field of dentistry does not only focus on an individual patient or clinician—rather, the goal is to provide a collaborative effort amongst dentists to provide comprehensive care for everyone. Yet I have also seen many ways in which dental services are highly lacking in communities around me. Drawing on my own transformative experiences from gaining a new smile, I would love to move outside of private practice to the larger, underserved community on a consistent basis to deliver care that not only improves oral health but fosters positive and trusting relationships as well. I envision myself working and serving the broader community around me: to do so with such a unique and impactful field as dentistry would be a great privilege.

* * *

Commentary:

This individual produced a beautifully written essay. It follows the common chronologic format: start with an early experience, followed by current dental experiences, and conclude with community involvement and future desires. The strongest part of this paper lies in the second half, where the writer reflects on building trust and meaningful connections in Asian InterVarsity, and how they apply to dental patients. I do wish the essay developed the theme of developing interpersonal trust further by including a concrete anecdote. —Dr. Watts

Author Bio:
- Andrew Ng
- University of Pittsburgh, Biological Sciences (Minor in Chemistry and Music), Class of 2016
- University of Pennsylvania School of Dental Medicine, Class of 2020
- "Throughout college, I participated in a select few activities into which I put a lot of time and effort, and really enjoyed. I invested most of my efforts into a Christian college ministry called Pitt Asian InterVarsity as a mentor and leader, which completely transformed my life. In addition, I was involved with the Pitt Dental Science Club (the pre-dental organization) as secretary and vice president, as well as a research lab at Pitt's dental school dedicated to genomic studies involving saliva. I was also a general chemistry lab TA, which turned out to be helpful when reviewing for the DAT. One piece of advice for pre-dental students is: always pursue your passion—you will gain so much by doing what you love, and it will give you a unique perspective on dentistry and life that no one else can take away from you."

3. ANTHONY'S ESSAY

I sit in the stiff wooden chair of the waiting room listening to the sounds coming from behind the office door. The waiting room of the dentist's office has always been my least favorite part of my trip due to its lack of excitement. I sit restless in my chair, waiting to be called into the next room. As the dentist turns the brass knob, the door slowly opens like the gradual parting of curtains on a stage and unveils what I believe to be the greatest symphony- melodic strumming of the scaler against one's teeth, the sweet, high-pitched whistling of the drill as it breaks the surface of the tooth, and the steady rattling of the wheels at the bottom of a chair as it swivels back and forth. There stands my grandfather in the doorway, the conductor of this symphony, dressed in a long, white coat with dental loupes hanging around his neck. For my entire life, I had admired my grandfather more than any other person; his ability to balance being both an excellent practicing dentist as well as a compassionate father, husband, uncle, and grandfather struck the deepest of chords in me.

From the moment I sat down in the chair, he was no longer my grandfather. The focused look in his eyes and attention he paid to my teeth, his favorite part of the human instrument, assured me there was not another thought going through his mind. I knew I wanted to be the man that I had admired so much but at such a young age I was unable to accomplish this. When my grandfather died, the music ceased. I had lost my grandfather and the dentist I had put so much faith and trust into. That was the day I knew dentistry would be the profession I would pursue. I wanted to be that man that, while sitting in the chair, countless people could place their trust in like I had done with my grandfather. He was the conductor of this perfectly harmonized symphony and I've aspired to take over that role.

As time went on, the sweet, melodic sounds of the dentist's office began to fade into the background of my everyday life. Not to say that my passion for dentistry had disappeared, but I no longer had anyone to conduct the music I loved so greatly. This all changed the first moment I walked into my shadowing internship at DP General Dentistry and as I was watching my first patient, I could hear the music again.

Through the many shadowing experiences I have had, I was able to acquire firsthand knowledge about the specialties in the dental field. I observed and learned the basics of dental implants and periodontal disease from Dr. James Pucci. I was able to see the sophisticated art of transforming one's smile in Dr. Kim's orthodontics office as well as the intricate procedures of oral surgery with Dr. Riccardo Ambrogio. However, my experiences at DP General Dentistry confirmed for me my love for dentistry and the music grew to a crescendo once again. The time I spent shadowing Dr. Ronald D'Andrea was much more than a dental shadowing experience, rather he taught me how to live a full life while practicing dentistry. He taught me how to foster a caring relationship with every patient that walks through the front door, one of confidence and trust, just as every musician has with their instrument. I was able to witness countless sighs of relief as he eased patients' pain, fixed a broken tooth, or simply removed a stain from the outer surface of a tooth, and I want to be the person who causes those sighs of relief someday. Dr. D'Andrea also talked about the importance of family in his life, a concept that resonated with me. He often stressed how important it is to find a balance between practicing dentistry and family and how both are necessary components to living a full life. I would often reflect on my own life during these conversations and realize how important family has been for me. Dentistry will allow me to fulfill my professional calling, having a family, and finding the balance between the two.

Although I have heard the tunes of many professions, dentistry is the only one that I find to be the most beautiful. I strongly desire to help people by treating and fostering wellness both physically and emotionally while being the family man that my grandfather was, whom I admire a great deal. Knowing that dentistry can enhance a person's life is something I find very rewarding and it is personally why I have chosen dentistry as my lifelong vocation; it is the beat to which I want strum the rest of my life.

* * *

Commentary:
The overarching unique music/symphony theme is quirky yet effective. What a wonderful anecdote about his "scary" grandfather who was a dentist and wanting to hear music again. He extends the analogy to the "music of dentistry" to weave his experiences together. We learn about his grandfather as a role model and other clinical practitioners he learned from along the way. Patient and family relationships seem very important to the writer, suggesting he will have compassion for future patients. Certain insights show the author to be a mature, contemplative individual, e.g. "countless people could place their trust in like I had done with my grandfather." Overall, this is a strong writer who has crafted a compelling personal statement. —Dr. Lian

Author Bio:
- Anthony DeFilippo
- Providence College, Biology and Psychology (Minor in Neuroscience), Class of 2016
- University of Connecticut School of Dental Medicine, Class of 2020
- "In college, I was a member of three honor society chapters: Alpha Epsilon Delta Pre-Professional Honor Society, of which I served as Treasurer for two years, Psi Chi Psychology Honor Society, and Sigma Xi Scientific Research Honor Society. I was the head researcher on Dr. Charles Toth's research team, where we worked primarily on stem cell research. I also completed three independent research studies in the Psychology department studying ADHD-like behaviors and the effects of time pressure on humans and spatial memory in rats. Outside the classroom, I served as president of the Pre-Dental Society, an Admissions Ambassador, and Honors Mentor, a mentoring program that allows upper class men to help and guide incoming freshman in the honors program."

4. DANIEL'S ESSAY

When I was very young, maybe four years old, my mother bought me a book entitled *Look Inside Your Body*. For some reason I grew enamored with the detailed diagrams and drawings of the human body. In retrospect, this book most likely piqued my attention because of the vivid colors. However, this interest in the colors and images soon translated into a curiosity about human anatomy. I read this book daily, and as I read I would trace the length of the digestive system or circulatory system with my fingers and try to locate these spots on my own body; I was trying to piece together the puzzle of how our bodies function.

Viewing these images of the body was the first time I thought about the human condition. As a young child, this book enabled me to accept that beyond the superficial facets of our existence, we are all simply pouches of bones and tissues. While this book illustrated the complexities and intricacies of the human body, it also showed me the fragility of the human species. Humans may dominate earth, but at our core, we are no more significant than an ant. However, though we are bound by the limits of our bodies, we are driven by the depth of our minds. Even though our bodies will inevitably break down, medical professionals use their limitless capacity to solve problems to help ameliorate limitations of anatomy.

My interest in dentistry developed during my junior year of high school. I had severe jaw pain towards the end of that year, but I decided to wait until after finals to go see a dentist. During my U.S. History Regents Exam the pain became so excruciating that I had to hand in my exam early (surprisingly, I received a perfect score on the exam despite this). My mother rushed me to the dentist and he referred us to an oral surgeon – all four of my wisdom teeth were impacted and had to be extracted immediately. Later that day, at the oral surgeon's office, I was enticed by the variety of ailments the patients in the waiting room had. I remember speaking to the doctor about dentistry, and I was fascinated by the depth and scope of the field. After the procedure, one of the dental assistants showed me the teeth that were removed. I felt as though I had been transported back to kindergarten, reading that book all over again. Looking at my teeth, I was amazed at how something so small, can have such a crucial function. For the first time I was able to witness how doctors use their knowledge to combat the breakdowns of our bodies. This tension between physical and abstract knowledge is what initially drew me to dentistry.

Despite the trauma of removing my wisdom teeth, the experience still compelled me to research dentistry. I was inspired to become an oral surgeon. I am drawn to oral surgery because it focuses on the medical aspect of dentistry, which I find to be most challenging and intriguing. However, I am also drawn to the manual and aesthetic aspects of dentistry and I hope to expand this interest. Dentists use their imaginative minds to resolve the many anomalies of our bodies. Through my shadowing and clinical experiences, I was also amazed at the emphasis dentists place on bedside manner. This further spurred my pursuit of a dental career because in addition to the scientific aspect of the discipline, I will also have the opportunity to utilize my business and interpersonal communication skills.

Recently, I was rummaging through my old desk to find a book to read to my nephew and beneath all the Dr. Seuss, I found the book that had sparked my interest in healthcare. The ripped edges and crayon marks did not faze him, he was instantly transfixed, and I saw my four year old self in him. I was reminded why I want to become a dentist: while human existence is marked with fragility, the limitlessness of our minds far surpasses our anatomical hindrances and I hope to join the ranks of those who devote their lives to lessening this disparity.

* * *

Commentary:

This is a solid and well written essay that smoothly addresses all the questions a personal statement should: Who is this applicant? How did they develop an interest in dentistry? Do they seem like an interesting person that can contribute hobbies and unique perspectives to the new dental class? The essay uses the tried-and-true technique of opening with an interesting motif or fact (the human body book) and loops back to it at the end, bringing the essay to a sincere conclusion. One weakness of the essay actually stems from one of its strengths. I liked how the bulk of the essay was the author's reflection and musings; however, it references nearly no extracurricular or research experience, related to dentistry or not, outside of a single encounter with the oral surgeon. —Dr. Yang

Author Bio:

- Daniel S. Nassimi
- New York University, Business Management and Organization (Minor in Chemistry), Class of 2016
- Columbia University College of Dental Medicine, Class of 2020
- "In college, I was highly involved in extracurricular activities; I was Vice President of the Pre-Dental-Outreach Club and Iranian Jewish Club, I did research at NYUCD, and volunteered/shadowed in various offices and specialties. In some ways I was a nontraditional applicant to dental school as I was a student at the NYU Stern School of Business; however I believe that my business degree endowed me with a dynamic skill set and allowed my application to stand out. Throughout the application process I was very proactive in networking with current dental students and faculty at the schools that I wanted to attend, and I believe this was the most crucial aspect of my application strategy that resulted in numerous acceptances."

5. ERIC'S ESSAY

It was March of 2010, and I was speaking on the phone with a mother of three through a Haitian Creole translator at Boston Medical Center. Within the last two months, I was able to help her secure an infant car seat for her new baby, apply for food stamps recertification, and complete an application for utility discounts through the Massachusetts Fuel Assistance program. Together, we had made considerable progress in improving the social determinants of her and her family's health. Yet that day she had called for a new reason; she had inquired about dental treatment. Growing up in Haiti, she had limited access to oral health care and only visited the dentist once for an emergency. She explained that persistent oral pain prevented her from adequately caring for her children, and asked if I would be able to connect her to a dental resource.

Though I did not perform dental procedures during my time volunteering as a patient advocate at the Women's Resource Center in Boston Medical Center, I performed an equally important role—connecting low-income patients, such as the mother above, to invaluable resources in order to improve their lifestyles and thus their health. From collaborating with medical providers, social workers, non-profits, and the patients themselves, I learned to develop excellent listening and interpersonal skills, as well as clinical professionalism, aiding to secure the best health outcomes possible for the patients I fought for. Although at times it was difficult troubleshooting the linguistic, logistical, and bureaucratic hurdles facing my team, I readily accepted these challenges and successfully navigated the complex landscape of insurance and health services to ensure my patients' utmost success in accessing better health outcomes. More importantly,

I gained considerable perspective on the social determinants of health that can have a significant impact on families.

From there I took my gained insights of patient advocacy and social initiative to the general dentistry practices of Dr. Liu in my hometown of Los Angeles where I shadowed and volunteered over the span one and a half years. Besides learning about the dental profession and assisting in a wide range of procedures, I quickly noticed parallels between Dr. Liu's work as a dentist and my work as a patient advocate. In particular, I found the strong relationships that he developed with his patients to be similar to the relationships I developed with my patients – relationships built upon health, fortified by a commitment to the greater good, and strengthened through mutual trust. As a result, I challenged myself to go beyond assisting dental procedures and learn not only about different insurance policies that shape the financial dynamics of dentistry, but also about patient lifestyles to provide the best oral care possible. Moreover, Dr. Liu showed me from his genuine patient care and fluid communication with assistants and office staff that dentists are equipped with an enhanced social conscience, a quality quintessential to dentistry that distinguishes the profession from other fields of healthcare.

Above all, my commitment to the best self and the common good sees tremendous alignment with my passion for dentistry. The creation of a patient's best self through oral health and projected confidence, and the commitment to the greater good from a public health perspective— these are my visions and aspirations in dentistry. Serving as Co-President of the Harvard College Red Cross further instilled within me the values of service to the common good. Under my leadership, the club now provides free monthly CPR and First Aid certification to members of the Cambridge community and teaches a newly established Community Disaster Education Program for Boston grade-school students. The unbelievable strength of a relationship that can empower and heal a patient through education and patient advocacy reinforces my belief in an individual influencing the greater good. My continuing journey with dentistry has centered these values as my moral compass.

After reviewing the Haitian Creole mother's insurance coverage and speaking with her insurers, I shared with her the fantastic news that she and her children were eligible for a number of dental benefits. Next, we scheduled an appointment at the Boston Medical Center dental clinic. The feeling of success in connecting her to oral care was undoubtedly rewarding, but more fulfilling will be the day I can care for patients like her as a dental professional.

* * *

Commentary

This essay is truly great. I particularly enjoy the introduction detailing the writer's work in aiding the Haitian woman and her family. He shows maturity, an awareness of the social determinants of health, and an understanding of complexity of the health care system that it takes others many years to appreciate. This applicant has an impressive background in many extracurricular activities in both scope and depth. As a reader, I get a sense that the writer is ready to hit the ground running and doesn't need to be educated extensively on social inequities, but instead is ready to make an impact. In general, it is clear that extensive reflection and editing led to this polished final product. —Dr. Kuhn

Author Bio:

- Eric Chen
- Harvard College, Molecular and Cellular Biology (Minor in Global Health and Health Policy), Class of 2012
- University of California School of Dentistry, Class of 2016
- "While academic excellence, leadership opportunities, research experience, and public service are undoubtedly important for dental school admissions, keep in mind that interviewers want to learn about the person behind all those accomplishments and accolades. Besides serving as a patient advocate, I also worked as a tour guide, cleaned bathrooms, and worked in a restaurant throughout college. Although these jobs were not the most glamorous, they were invaluable for my personal growth. Interviewers were keen to ask me about how my work experiences shaped me into the individual I was."

6. HANNAH'S ESSAY

My hand slowly brushes across the wall, helping me navigate down the endless hallway. My head is spinning and my mind starts to go blank. I feel a handle to what I hope is a bathroom, quickly shut the door behind me, and slowly slip to the floor. The next few minutes disappear into nothingness, and shortly after, I start to regain awareness of my surroundings. I try to think back as to why I am sitting on the floor of a bathroom with sweaty hands and a rapid heartbeat. I freshen up and head back into the hallway, walking until I reach the room where the surgeon continued to work.

Although I have worked in my father's orthodontic office and shadowed for years, this was my first experience in an oral surgery office. I had walked into the operatory just as the procedure started, completely unaware of what was about to unfold. Now more collected, I watched as the experienced hands of the surgeon cut a full arch flap of the patient's edentulous maxilla. He placed a series of implants so the man could once again take pleasure in eating, speaking, and smiling. Caught at first by surprise, I was immersed in the rest of the procedure.

Dentistry has been a part of my life for as long as I can remember —I began filing charts in my father's office soon after mastering the alphabet. My mother was also involved in healthcare as my twin brother, Zach, and I were growing up. She took on the role of a navigator for seriously ill friends and family, helping steer them through the health care maze for cancer treatment. By example, my parents showed me how I can make a difference in someone's life. As a naturally curious child, I would always ask them why some people had medical aliments but others did not. Some of these questions were small and personal: why did I need speech therapy but Zach did not? Other questions were much larger, even global.

My family traveled to India for a wedding when I was twelve. Against the lavish wedding backdrop, we were surrounded by extreme poverty. I saw children with clothes held together by a thread and expressions that could elicit empathy in even the most cold-hearted person. I hated feeling powerless, and desperately wanted to do something, anything to help. That trip ignited my passion for service and it became a catalyst for my desire to make a difference.

Later that year, I went with my family to a remote Peruvian village, where part of our project included giving oral health instructions. Many of the adults had large, toothless grins, because the only dental option available was extraction. The children, however, still had time. Despite the language barrier, we were able to effectively teach basic hygiene, evident by their eagerness to use their new toothbrushes during our stay. I learned that helping people not only had the capacity to improve their lives, but could also change mine: I began to understand the difference between real problems and "first world" problems. This transition from watching to doing gave me a sense of pride and accomplishment knowing I could make an impact. Limited in projects I could participate in, but eager to become involved, I volunteered as an EMT as soon as I met the age requirements.

Ultimately, however, I knew my impact would be through dentistry. In addition to shadowing general dentists, and assisting with patient care, unit preparation, and lab work, I have also observed almost every specialty. These experiences during high school and college have exposed me to the vast spectrum of the profession, from root canals to botox injections. Outside of a private setting, I have also helped provide dental care in inner city St. Louis and rural Honduras, as well as helped build a clean water system in Ghana.

In my father's office, the offices I shadowed, and the clinics I worked in locally and abroad, I found a special connection between the dentist and the patient. Through dentistry, I have experienced a sense of trust, understanding, compassion, and friendship. These one-on-one relationships, combined with the technical marvels of dentistry, have made my career path clear.

I have always been ambitious, whether it be through leading a service trip to Ghana, overcoming my fear of heights on the world's largest canyon swing in New Zealand, or volunteering here in St. Louis. I am committed to a dental career, and confident that not only can I handle the rigors of dental school, but that I also have the heart and humor that go hand in hand with that commitment.

* * *

Commentary:
One of the foundational aspects of every personal statement is that it should be "personal": it should showcase both the author's individual experiences and his or her personality, strengths, and even vulnerabilities. The author does this very well. It's challenging to admit vulnerability, but doing so can set apart an applicant from the majority of essays that showcases only the writer's strengths. Sharing both her queasiness in the first paragraph and helplessness and "first world problems" later on, the author comes across as relatable and genuine. One thing that could have strengthened this essay would be a deeper dive into one specific overseas trip instead of briefly mentioning many, such as by describing specific impact and contributions the writer had.—Dr. Liu

Author Bio:
- Hannah Jenkins
- Washington University in St. Louis, Psychology, Class of 2016
- University of Michigan School of Dentistry, Class of 2020
- "During college, I was involved in a variety of community service projects through Global Brigades, Alpha Phi Omega, and my sorority, Kappa Delta. I also participated in psychology research and played club lacrosse in my free time. I am a firm believer that a dental school application is more than just your GPA and DAT numbers, and that a well written, well edited personal statement can make a big difference. Don't be afraid to get feedback from friends and family!"

7. HELEN'S ESSAY

Blessed with nimble fingers, a bright smile, and an eager-to-learn attitude, Theresa was my best piano student. I had spent a whole summer volunteering at Bethel Foster Home, the only orphanage in China dedicated to caring for blind orphans. Even though they were abandoned by their birthparents and cannot see the world, these children were still some of the most joyous people I'd ever met. The moment that Theresa mastered "Heart and Soul" with two hands (no easy feat even for a sighted beginner) gave us both an incredible sense of accomplishment. Other than teaching piano, I also guided the children on excursions, fed the little ones, and taught older girls to make jewelry, a skill that will be useful once they are old enough to leave the orphanage. My time at Bethel was truly meaningful, and it reinforced my passion to help those who are marginalized or ignored by society to reach their highest potential.

For years, I thought medicine would be my life's calling; helping people regain their health and normal life by applying the knowledge of healing really resonated with me. I was inspired by Dr. Paul Farmer and Dr. Jim Kim's dedication to treating tuberculosis, addressing social inequities, and fighting for the rights of marginalized peoples. I aspired to be like them.

The mouth first caught my attention freshman year when I was on the job as a Harvard Crimson science reporter. The story was that researchers connected obesity to higher risks of periodontal disease. The news struck me as interesting because, as a keen pre-medical student, I had been so fascinated by diseases such as obesity and cancer that I sub- consciously saw the mouth as detached from the body. A little research quickly proved my perception wrong: severe oral diseases can lead to significant health problems.

Studying the history and sociology of dental care has given me a unique lens to view the issues dentists face today. One of the biggest challenges is ensuring access to dental care to disadvantaged regions. Society has long recognized the important role of physicians in public health, but dentists rose to prominence only a few centuries ago. The importance of oral health is often overlooked by both regular people and policy makers, especially since oral diseases are inherently so prevalent and do not demand immediate attention. Once I started to pay attention, I noticed that many people's malnutrition and other illnesses could be traced to their neglected teeth. I also recognized that poor dentition is a cause for social stigma. At Bethel, I got to know an adorable boy who had a cleft lip, and it saddens me to know he might remain marginalized by society because of a condition fixable by a $500 surgery. Back at Harvard, I became actively involved in fundraising efforts that supported more than fifteen orphans' surgeries. If I can bring joy to the Bethel children with my piano and beading skills, I know I can make an even more tangible difference as a dentist and address this often unmet yet overlooked need.

I became sure that dentistry is the right path for me when I gained exposure to its daily workings last summer. From shadowing general dentists to an oral surgeon, I learned a great deal about common dental procedures, how to interact with patients and put them at ease, and the business aspects of running a practice. I found the fact that dentists produce concrete results in just one or two visits appealing, and this fits in with my goal of one day starting mobile dental clinics in underprivileged communities. I also love that dentists work with their hands so extensively. I am the girl known for spending hours at a time making jewelry or building elaborate origami kusudama. Working on patients' teeth is a much more intricate and meaningful craft, one that I can see myself happily practicing.

As a little girl, I dreamt of being the next James Bond—until my hopes were dashed at the tender age of nine upon learning that MI6 doesn't recruit Canadian citizens. Over the years, my intellectual pursuits and career aspirations have matured, but my fundamental motivation has not changed. I believe that meaning in life comes from using one's abilities to champion a cause and to leave the greatest impact. To me, becoming a dentist is not just for the career. Promoting oral health is such a noble humanitarian goal, and I know that dentistry would offer me a niche to realize my potential to make the biggest difference.

* * *

Commentary:

This essay shows excellent balance between showing and telling. The author highlights valuable skills for a successful dentist and the anecdotes she chooses are illustrative. Her experiences at the orphanage (through details such as jewelry making and feeding young children) left so much of an impact on her that she took a meaningful event to the next level. The essay shows her to be resourceful, compassionate, and craving to make an impact in the world. Also, injecting a playful anecdote can be difficult to do in a personal statement, but the author weaves her humor in well as she concludes with her dreams of being the next 'James Bond' thwarted by what may be so seemingly trivial as one's citizenship status. —Sangita Murali

Author Bio:
- Helen Yang
- Harvard College, History of Science (Minor: Global Health and Health Policy), Class of 2012
- Harvard School of Dental Medicine, Class of 2016
- "A college admissions officer once told me that colleges look for two types of applicants: Well rounded and Very Pointy (exceptional in one field). Dental schools are no different. I've always had a very wide interests and activities, from global health to journalism to teaching, so I made sure my application reflected my well-roundedness as well as how my diverse interests relates to dentistry. For example, my senior thesis focused on the modern history of tooth whitening and role of American dentists played in promoting the idea of white teeth being healthy and normal. It was the topic of a lively discussion at many of my interviews, especially with the older faculty members."

8. JAIME'S ESSAY

Dentistry is my first career choice. In some ways, it also reflects my second and third career choices. A chemistry researcher is precise and meticulous. An educator is analytical and innovative. As an aspiring dentist, I see myself integrating the elements of both professions. A career in dentistry allows me a platform to improve policies in the community and provide quality care. I want to master the skills of dental treatment, build rapport with my peers, and educate my patients to cultivate exceptional oral health.

Growing up, I had a fervent passion for chemistry and wanted to be recognized as an accomplished scientist. To me, performing a successful chemistry experiment involves persistent repetition and resilient attention to each procedural step: calibrating gel filtration columns, generating plasmid sequences, and employing membrane-permeable crosslinkers. Today, my pursuit is different but the principle is the same. My interest in dentistry blossomed when I experienced a facial deformity in which my right maxillary canine was dislodged above my other teeth. My childhood dentist thoroughly explained her method of operating on my "vampire tooth". Expand the socket. Breach the ligament. Clamp tightly, and pull. She explained to me each and every procedural step to the grain and constantly reassured me that her treatment would be successful. My admiration for her ran deep as she influenced my belief in treatment and restoration of my smile. I grew fascinated with the idea of performing dental treatment and instilling faith and confidence in others. I credit Dr. Lynn for planting a seed in my garden of aspirations.

To further explore my interest in dentistry, I've had the fortunate opportunity to volunteer as a dental assistant and dental radiologist in Dr. Lim's office. Dr. Lim introduced me to numerous techniques and procedures: fillings, sealants, and extractions. During my time, I familiarized myself with many day-to-day activities: taking X-rays on patients, sterilizing equipment, and taking alginate impressions. Although these were valuable things to learn, the most important aspect of dentistry, of course, is patient care. At his office, I came into contact with a diverse group of patients, each with their own set of dental needs and problems. Every individual that entered his office had unique preferences on how they wished to be performed. I observed as Dr. Lim catered to each individual needs to the best of his ability and established mutual trust and confidence between his patients. Dr. Lim's exceptional accommodation to their needs empowered them to take control of their own oral health. Through his example, my interest in dentistry evolved into a passion as I began to recognize elements of my prior experiences being incorporated into a fulfilling profession.

Beyond elements of acute precision and patient care, I am drawn to dentistry for another reason. I enjoy cultivating an amiable environment and exploring ideas with my peers. Upon completing my second year in university, I've participated as a member of Dr. Vas' research group. Working under her tutelage has reinforced my appreciation for discovery and education and it has placed me in a position with like-minded individuals. Her persistence and expectations have improved my ability to think analytically and create new ideas. As I took ownership of a project involving conformational studies of apolipoprotein E, I was able to initiate changes that optimized the efficiency of our experiments. These skills have created a foundation for me to continue in dentistry. I believe the key to expanding oral health lies in education and research. As I seek to become an advocate in my profession, I hope to be involved in improving the processes we use everyday. These include refining protocols for our treatment, extending overall healthcare, and expanding our field of work. Through extensive study and research, I hope to inform my peers and advocate my opinion on policies to improve our standard of practicing dentistry.

I choose to pursue a career in dentistry after following a circuitous path. My relationship with previous mentors has motivated me to enter a field where I can find endless joy in treating dental deformities and instilling confidence in others. As I seek to become a skillful practitioner, an inspiring educator, and a respected professional in my career, I believe a career in dentistry will fulfill my personal and professional goals.

* * *

Commentary:

This personal statement is a good example of a thoughtful and organized approach to writing. He declares his mission and goals in dentistry in the opening paragraph and then expands upon in subsequent paragraphs. As a reader, I can create a personality profile in my mind and helps me consider how this person would perform in dental school and mesh with classmates. He comes across as intelligent, hard-working, and analytical. This essay's greatest weakness is the lack of warmth in the voice and straightforward writing style, and I recommend the author convey more of his personality through telling stories. —Dr. Lu

Author Bio:
- Jaime Tran
- California State University Long Beach, Class of 2016
- University of California Los Angeles School of Dentistry, Class of 2020
- "Before dental school, I was involved in a biochemistry research lab that studied Apolipoprotein E. I was also a tutor and teacher for many science and math courses. I had a few years of exposure to the dental profession through my dental assisting and radiology ROP course and I shadowed my local dentist. During my free time, I enjoyed playing basketball, playing billiards, mini-golfing, and going out for food adventures."

9. JAYNE'S ESSAY

Last summer, while shadowing in a prosthodontist's office, one small sign stood out to me from all of the wall décor that read, "Dentists help the world smile." Although this pithy statement is admittedly somewhat cliché, I believe it encompasses my desire to be a dentist because each word reminds me why I am right for this challenging and rewarding profession. I want to build relationships with patients, bringing commitment and compassion to the field of dentistry. I want to be a dentist because I want to help the world smile.

Dentists. Dentistry has always been familiar to me because my dad is an orthodontist; it was his work that initially piqued my interest in the profession. I believe that dentistry is a good fit for me because it utilizes my scientific mind and motor skills, gives opportunities for interaction with people, and allows for balance with family and other interests. Furthermore, it will challenge me to orchestrate a team, similar to the teamwork required for playing volleyball at Hope College, which culminated in a NCAA Division III National Championship last year. Many years of athletic experience have taught me about teamwork, commitment, leadership, efficient use of time, overcoming challenges, and performing under pressure – all attributes of an excellent dentist.

Dentists *help.* One way that I discovered my love for service was by volunteering at Health Intervention Services, a non-profit, faith-based health center located in West Michigan. I was able to help many uninsured people by assisting the dentist in the clinic, resulting in grateful smiles and relief from dental ailments. I was motivated by seeing how a dental education combined with a heart for missions and knowledge of the Spanish language could be used together to help those in need, right in my neighborhood. I realized that I want my life to revolve around helping people. However, missions and volunteering are not the only way that I will be able to serve others as a dentist; I believe that I can also use my passion for teaching. As long as I remember, I wanted to be a teacher. Through tutoring college students in chemistry and biology, I have been able to convey my knowledge to others in ways they can understand and apply themselves. As a dentist, perhaps by teaching academic material at least part time, or certainly in a dental office setting, I will be able to teach people how to live healthier lives.

Dentists help *the world*. I discovered my deep passion for the Spanish language and culture in high school, but studying abroad in Spain for a semester in college taught me more than any class could. This adventurous step completely submerged me in a culture different from my own, exposing me to global issues such as poverty. By living with a Spanish family for five months, I saw life from a brand-new perspective; by stepping out of my comfort zone, I developed independence. Furthermore, I increased my proficiency in a language that will allow me to connect with the large and growing Hispanic population living in my own community, as well as those in other countries. My experience in Brazil on a medical mission boat birthed my interest in the possibility of taking time away from a regular practice to perform missionary dentistry in underserved areas around the world.

Dentists help the world *smile*. While observing the prosthodontist, I saw one particularly notable procedure: she completed several anterior composite resin restorations, which completely transformed a woman's smile in about an hour. I loved seeing how overjoyed the woman was when she left – it was an instant reward for the work. Although orthodontics is a longer process, I have experienced firsthand that the outcome leaves the patient smiling bigger and with more confidence than ever before. While these results are very aesthetic, many patients leave their dentist with more pressing health problems solved. While in Brazil, I saw desperate patients leave with joy after their dental pain was relieved. Dentistry is empowering. Smiles are contagious, and my goal is to bring smiles to as many people as possible.

I want to live for something greater than myself, intentionally loving others and living a story of meaning. I have a calling in this world to make a contribution, and I am excited to contribute to the lives of many people by improving their dental health. I am looking forward to going to dental school in order to achieve my mission: I will help the world smile.

* * *

Commentary:
The unique structure of this essay helps it stand out. Whether prospective applicants choose to adopt a similar setup is up to his risk tolerance, as it may come across as gimmicky to some readers. That said, the author uses this framework effectively to showcase her interest in dentistry as well as her own strengths in a systematic and thorough manner. The essay manages to cover a lot of ground and weaves in her diverse experiences (volleyball, clinic volunteering, study abroad in Spain, shadowing a prosthodontist, mission trip to Brazil) seamlessly in a way that is effortless to read about, avoiding the common mistake of appearing to reciting a CV. —Dr. Liu

Author Bio:
- Jayne Kessel
- Hope College, Chemistry and Spanish, Class of 2016
- University of Michigan School of Dentistry, Class of 2020
- "My biggest time commitment prior to dental school was playing varsity volleyball all four years of undergrad. I barely did any research, so I made up for that with a 4.0 GPA, high DAT scores, and other shadowing, volunteering, and academic involvements. I believe it's better to pour your time into things you're interested in and to do those things well than to do something "just because it would look good on an application." The things that shaped me the most during undergrad were studying abroad and playing a sport, neither of which has anything to do with dentistry at first glance."

10. JESSICA'S ESSAY

Passion is a powerful emotion like love, joy, hatred or anger; science and art are my passion. I look toward dentistry as being my passion. My fondest memory of the dentist was as a child. My appointment had finished and I ran to smile for my cavity-free photo. I remember looking at the Wall of Smiles and thinking, "One day, I want to help people smile like me."

Through grade school I considered many professions; pianist, architect and dentist came to mind. However, dentistry was the sole profession that incorporated all professional qualities into one. A pianist, like a dentist, requires stamina to complete a song or a procedure. They train their feet to alter the tone of a song, and their hands to control the speed and volume. A dentist rotates the hand piece by foot control all while performing precise manipulations with the hands. Like a pianist, a dentist creates art.

At the age of six, I began to develop my manual dexterity by playing piano. I explored many musical styles and was the youngest entrepreneur in my town in 2005. I created a successful music school-production company which developed a not-for-profit division to help raise money for underprivileged students and awareness about the importance of music for youth. Here, I was nominated as one of Canada's "Top 20 Under 20." Now, I plan to promote awareness about oral health issues in local communities. Music will forever be in my heart, but is it science and art in dentistry that awards me a greater passion.

To me, dentistry is the architecture of the mouth, where each tooth is a building. Caries of a tooth require drilling and filling as a building requires excavation and restoration. Just as landscaping improves visual appeal to a building, flossing and brushing help maintain oral hygiene. The decision to pursue dentistry was simple: it combined both art and science.

I became seriously interested in dentistry after shadowing my dentist on career day. I later worked as a receptionist for five years, in addition to observing procedures such as root canals, fillings and crowns. As a receptionist I learned how to bill patients, process insurance claims, book appointments, but importantly learned to build relationships with patients. I furthered my knowledge and interest in dentistry as part of the Pre-Dental Society at The University of Western Ontario (UWO) for five years; two of which as Vice-President. I helped students on their journey and became aware of potentially teaching dentistry upon graduation.

Having an interest in dentistry is but one part of my goal, the other is to have the drive to accomplish the goal. Many have called me determined, motivated and passionate, but it is perseverance that sets me apart. I stay optimistic in life because I have been challenged with difficult events. My mother's illnesses, my cousin's suicide, and a learning disability diagnosed late in my university career were three strenuous but manageable obstacles.

My mother was diagnosed with a brain injury and bipolar mental illness. In January 2007, she fainted while driving and hit a school bus. During summer of 2008, she experienced psychosis and did not believe that I was her daughter. During this time, I developed limitless patience.

May 2007, my cousin—age 15—committed suicide because she was bullied. I was her Holy Confirmation Sponsor and her loss was painful for me. At this time, I was a Residence Coordinator at UWO for Orientation Week 2007. I was inspired to raise awareness about Words That Hurt through workshops to educate the Orientation leaders.

In grade school, I was offered admission into a gifted program as my science, visual and spatial abilities were superior; but, my comprehension ability was average. In time, this stunted my learning until summer of 2008. Once diagnosed, I applied specific techniques to strengthen my study habits thereby increasing my GPA. Although mentally exhausted in my second and third years, my later successes confirm my ability to handle the rigorous course load offered in dental school.

These difficult events along with the many positive experiences I have encountered define my life and prepare me for future success. I believe I am an excellent candidate for dental school because I have persevered. Today, I look to you to help me take the next step in my life and to fulfill my passion of becoming a dentist. No one can say it better than Dr. Seuss, my favourite author, "Today is your day! Your mountain is waiting. So...get on your way."

* * *

Commentary:
This essay stands out because of its intimate subject matter, which differs from those of more traditional personal statements. On the surface, these personal, difficult happenings in her life seem neither interrelated or relevant to dentistry. However, taken together, they paint a vivid picture of an introspective, optimistic, smart, and determined young woman and explain how overcoming these challenges have shaped her into the person she is today. —Dr. Yang

Author Bio:
- Jessica E. Metcalfe
- Western University, Canada, Biology (Minor in Medical Sciences), Class of 2010
- Boston University Henry M. Goldman School of Dental Medicine, Class of 2015
- "My extracurriculars included: flag football, being a frosh leader for three years, pre-dental society executive committee and owning my own music school. I took 5 years to complete my degree as I changed programs a couple of times. This gave me the opportunity to explore other courses such as history of rock 'n' roll and Italian language. In my last year, I completed an undergraduate thesis where I now have a published paper. Attending BU was an opportunity of a lifetime and I am so very grateful! Today, I get to look back at my 14-year-old self and say, "you're a dentist"!"

II. JESSIE'S ESSAY

My interest in dentistry doesn't stem from a lifelong love affair or a single epiphanic moment. That's not how most people find their dream job anyway—it's usually less dramatic. Choosing a career requires careful consideration and preparation, and it's hard to strike the perfect fit while balancing personal aspirations, core values, and unique skills. But it can be done, and this is the story of how I became passionate about a career where I can use my own skills to enable others to live healthy lives.

The starting point for my career choice was simple: I knew I wanted to work in a field where I would be helping other people on a daily basis. Though every job has tasks that need be completed by the end of the day, not every job holds a lot of intrinsic meaning. I wanted my hard work to directly help people, and with my penchant for the natural sciences, it didn't take long for me to be drawn to patient care.

I decided to start shadowing dental clinics to see what kind of work I was getting into. I learned about the different procedures that dentists typically perform as well as some of the challenges of running a business and dealing with patients. But most of all, I saw firsthand the impact that dental care has on an individual's quality of life. I remember one day watching a middle-aged man carefully pull off his partial denture to reveal a mouth gaping with holes. As the dentist pulled out one of his few remaining teeth, I struggled to imagine how long he must have gone with inadequate dental care, and I felt compelled to help him. Through shadowing dental clinics, I realized that choosing dentistry would definitely enable me to fulfill my life goal of helping others.

I think it's empathy that also drives me to another source of inspiration: I'm pursuing dentistry because I want to build close, long-term relationships with others. As a patient, I greatly value my relationship with my dentist, who I started seeing for semi-annual checkups when I was seven. With every checkup, he told me my teeth looked great and I gave him the latest updates on my life. As I got to know my dentist better over the years, he made me feel like I was more than just a patient, and because of that I trusted his decisions more. Now, reflecting on what I want from my own career, I realize that I greatly value the opportunity to cultivate humanizing, intimate relationships.

Ideology and inspiration aside though, I know that pursuing a career means I must also look at its more practical aspects. For example, it takes excellent manual dexterity to be a good dentist. Lucky for me, this is a great fit with the technical skills I've been developing since I was young. Playing the piano was a huge part of my life throughout my childhood, and to this day, I still love working with my hands. When I attended a drill-and-fill lab with my university's Dental Science Club, I really enjoyed doing the cavity preparation and filling simulation. Dental work and music may sound like an odd combination, but I know that I can make the most of my skills through the fine-tuned handiwork and artistry that dentistry requires.

More recently, I've also been working on becoming a better leader, which can help make my dental aspirations a reality. Dentists often have their own businesses, and it takes strong leadership skills to run a practice that produces results. As president of my university's Chinese American Students Association, I've planned, budgeted, and advertised for big events like our annual Lunar New Year Festival, where over three hundred people got the chance to enjoy live cultural performances and sample traditional Chinese food. I've learned how to delegate work and mediate conflicts, but more importantly, I've learned that effective leadership adapts to the unique strengths of a group. My future goal is to create a practice where all my team members can make the most of their technical and interpersonal skills, so that our team can provide patients with the best care possible.

Choosing to pursue dentistry hasn't been an easy process; it's taken a lot of time, thought, and reflection. Though it may not be the most exciting story, for me, the careful consideration that I've invested in my career choice makes it all the more meaningful. I'm confident I have made the right choice.

* * *

Commentary:
There isn't always a eureka! moment. Sometimes our strongest convictions arise from simmering over time. This essay is a notable example of just that. Despite lacking a grand opening, the author is able to demonstrate many great qualities including a mature voice, a strong degree of introspection, and a clear organized approach. By the close of the first paragraph, it is apparent to the reader that this will be a thoughtful approach to understand the many subtleties of dentistry and the importance of relationship-building. One point to note is to be aware of the phrasing of "dealing with patients," as if patients are often burdensome. It can be rewritten as "working with patients" to be more neutral. Overall, this is a solidly written essay that achieves its purpose.
—Dr. Lu

Author Bio:
- Jessie Jiang
- University of Pittsburgh, Chemistry and Economics, Class of 2016
- University of California Los Angeles School of Dentistry, Class of 2020
- "Before dental school, I was involved in academic and cultural extracurricular activities. I was a TA for general chemistry recitation for 3 years, and I completed three years of research in a chemistry lab. I was also very involved with my school's Chinese American Students Association, as well as the Asian community at large. Before committing to dentistry as a career path, I was pre-med and spent many hours volunteering at the university hospital. Later, I got the chance to shadow several dentists."

12. JOSEPH'S ESSAY

"Hot Crossed Buns" and "Heart and Soul" – the first pieces my hands coaxed from our upright grand piano. Rudimentary, yes, but it was a start. I was elated at my budding ability, and my eight-year-old heart was already set on its next goal: Gershwin's "Rhapsody in Blue." Yet I quickly realized that learning to play a masterpiece would require much more than desire; it would require time and effort. My hands were novice and untrained, but they were determined. I practiced scales, memorized music theory, and eventually learned to harmonize the efforts of both my hands and feet. Now, after fifteen years of practicing, those same hands can play not only Gershwin, but also Rachmaninov, Debussy, and Chopin. They have regularly accompanied a weekly congregation of several hundred churchgoers as they sang Sunday hymns. They know how to learn and are determined do hard things.

I was first introduced to dentistry in my father's Oral and Maxillofacial Surgery practice, where I prepared surgical rooms, sterilized instruments, and gently guided dizzy patients to the recovery room. I marveled at my father's skilled, miraculous hands and their ability to turn pain into relief. A desire seeded within me to use my hands for the same purpose. Yet, wanting to forge my own path, I decided as a freshman to major in business management. I began to immerse myself in learning the ways of the corporate world. I delved deep into my notebooks, learning the principles of accounting, marketing, and finance. As a vice president for the BYU Marketing Association, I created advertisements to publicize upcoming lectures and events.

I would find greater purpose over the next two years during my proselytizing mission in the Czech Republic and Slovakia. I had grown up doing service projects with the Boy Scouts of America and with my church youth group; but it was there, halfway across the world, that I learned what service truly is. Beyond physical service, my hands learned the changing power of compassionate service – as they closed around the shoulder of Luděk, who had previously intended suicide and needed the comfort to know that tomorrow would be better; as they wrote letters corresponding with Tomáš, a prisoner who was trying to change and needed to know that someone still believed in him; as they helped Zdeněk throw away his cigarettes, his eyes glistening with triumph. I learned greater sympathy while lifting others whose life experiences were vastly different from my own.

After those years of service I returned to studying business management, but I quickly discovered that my hands were not satisfied typing on a keyboard and clicking a mouse. My mind repeatedly returned to my father's hands those years growing up. They were filled with purpose, and the results of their service were immediately visible in the lives and faces of his patients. I continued to pursue my degree in business management, knowing that I could use those skills to successfully market a dental practice, strategically handle its finances, and effectively communicate with patients and employees. But after months of deliberation and discussion, my mind and hands were resolute – they were fixated on dentistry.

My hands itch to work, to create, to lift. They have always found joy in developing and expressing artistic ability – painting watercolor portraits in soft shades of pastel, carving and polishing a robin redbreast from wood, digitally illustrating cartoons for children's books. Recently, I have delved into the artistic side of dentistry by carving teeth and crowns out of wax in a dental lab techniques course. But beyond creating, my hands long to heal. For my Eagle Scout project, I travelled to Mexico for a week with Amigos de los Niños, a charity providing free services and hearing aids to children from low-income families. Words cannot capture the feeling as I helped place hearing aids on a six-year-old girl who grinned as she heard her mother's voice for the first time. I now love volunteering at the Share a Smile foundation, where I can help the poor and needy experience the joy of a clean, pain-free smile.

To me, dentistry is where art and healthcare converge to create both beauty and function. My hands are diligent, compassionate, and artistic. They are determined to pursue dentistry. The coming years will be challenging as my hands learn the art of this profession. But I know what it takes to get from "Hot Crossed Buns" to "Rhapsody in Blue" – and I am eager to begin.

* * *

Commentary:

Since application readers are tasked with a high volume to review, writers have little time to make a strong first impression. This essay's opening paragraph establishes an interesting narrative. The author is clearly a strong writer, with nice variation in sentence length and syntax. I am impressed by descriptions of mission work in Eastern Europe and Mexico and appreciate the recurring motif of hand skills. One weakness is that some parts of the third and fifth paragraph come across as overwritten and overly dramatic ("Words cannot capture the feeling" and "My hands learned the changing power"). It is challenging to walk a fine line between describing a meaningful interaction and praising one's own actions. —Dr. Lu

Author Bio:
- Joseph Mullen
- Brigham Young University, Business Management: Marketing, Class of 2016
- University of California Los Angeles School of Dentistry, Class of 2020
- "I believe I was a competitive applicant due to my strong academics, community service, and unique life experiences. In addition to volunteering at a dental clinic for the homeless, I was active in serving in my church congregation and mentoring elementary school youth. As mentioned in my personal statement, I took a 2-year gap in my university education to serve a mission for my church in the Czech Republic. I also worked as a Czech language teacher and did a marketing internship with a private medical practice. My hobbies included singing, piano playing, ballroom dancing, watercolor painting, and spending time with my wife (who was pregnant at the time)."

13. KAI'S ESSAY

My predental journey has been an amazing ride. I've had the privilege to meet wonderful individuals through volunteering and organized dentistry. My ultimate goal is to start a foundation that provides free dental care to low income and uninsured patients. I also want to stay involved with organized dentistry and hope to one day inspire my colleagues to join my volunteering cause.

I arrived at UCF unsure of my career path. Initially I chose to major in Electrical Engineering because it was familiar. I hoped it would spark the same interest it did in my sister. When I was in high school, I built a homemade laser pointer using leftover parts from a blue ray player. It was strong enough to burn through paper and light matches on fire. While the concepts of engineering still fascinate me, I eventually turned to a career I would enjoy more fully on the day-to-day: dentistry. In many ways, I can still apply the analytical skill and critical thinking that I've acquired from engineering. When engineers design a circuit board, they consider various methods before deciding on the one that best meets their requirements, much like dentists individualize care for their patient's needs and interests. Furthermore, I hope to incorporate my engineering background into dentistry to develop new technology that improves the ease and accessibility of care.

In 2011, I joined the Pre-Dental Student Association at UCF. It was a pivotal decision, as it helped me better define my interests in dentistry. I had the privilege to start volunteering at local dental clinics through the Dental Care Access Foundation and the Florida Hospital Community Impact. Both non-profit organizations recruit volunteer dentists to provide free dental care to underprivileged areas of Orlando. The dentists generously donate their time and skills to serve the less fortunate. Their genuine interest to give back ignited my own passion toward the field, and inspired me to follow in their footsteps.

This past year, as President of the UCF Pre-Dental Student Association, I wrote a donation proposal that reached local dentists and companies, like Crest Oral B. We received more than four thousand toothbrushes and toothpastes in response. With the supplies we raised and the partnerships we developed with local dentists, we traveled to local public schools in underprivileged areas of Orlando twice a month. We taught children about oral hygiene, provided fluoride treatment, and handed out complimentary dental hygiene kits.

One such trip to Ivey Lane Elementary particularly touched my heart. I taught an eight-year-old girl how to properly brush and floss her teeth. I asked her how many times a day you need to brush: she showed me "one" with her finger. I was surprised by her response because usually I'd hear some silly, large numbers... but one? She explained to me it was because her family doesn't have enough toothpaste. My heart sank, as I immediately began to fill her bag with extra toothbrushes and pastes. Moments like this are the reason I want to start a foundation, because no child should have to worry about not having enough toothpaste.

Last year, I became a predental member of the American Student Dental Association (ASDA). There, I had the opportunity to meet Jason Watts, the 2014-15 National Vice President of ASDA. After hearing him speak, I immediately became thrilled with organized dentistry. My "ASDA fever" grew after attending ASDA's district meetings, National Leadership Conference, and Annual Session. Attending these conferences as a predental student gave me new perspective. I learned to appreciate the strength and integrity of a united organizational front. I was recently appointed to serve as the 2015-16 National Predental Consultant for ASDA. My duties include informing councils about topics and issues related to predental students and serving as the liaison between the Predental Advisory Committee and the Council on Membership. I've learned to work well in a team, and I understand the importance of adapting different personalities in order to yield the best result as a team. Looking towards the rest of my term, I hope to provide further benefits and resources to predental students across the nation.

Being a non-traditional student, it has taken me longer to reach my career goals. However, I have enjoyed the journey. ASDA, my predental peers, and the amazing people that I volunteer with have truly ensured me that dentistry is the right path for me.

* * *

Commentary:
The author of the essay illustrates a strong pre-dental background that shows his deliberate efforts to step outside of his engineering background and join the pre-dental world by meeting so many people. He is ambitious and positive, leaving the reader eager to learn more about his motivation for starting a foundation to support the oral care needs of low income populations. Without saying it directly, we get a sense that the author is a team player who is excited to advance the field through a hands-on approach, although several parts of the essay toes the line of 'rehashed resume.' What the author could do to make this essay even stronger would be connecting how the he chose dentistry from engineering to show his sincere passion for dentistry rather than describing dental activities on his resume. —Sangita Murali

Author Bio:
- Kai Huang
- University of Central Florida, Electrical Engineering, Class of 2016
- University of Alabama at Birmingham, Class of 2020
- "I consider myself as a non-traditional predental student, as I spent 6 years to complete my engineering degree while fulfilling dental school application requirements. I was born and raised in Taiwan and immigrated to Florida in 2006. I struggled with the language barrier during my high school years; it was the toughest part of my life. What doesn't kill you makes your stronger right? I am passionate about organized dentistry and leadership. During my undergraduate years, I was fortunate to serve a number of leadership roles ranging from an officer to the president of Pre-Dental Student Association at UCF, District 5 Predental Planning Committee and ASDA National Predental Consultant."

14. LILY'S ESSAY

I confess that my path towards deciding on dentistry did not begin with a fixation on teeth. When my first tooth fell out, I admittedly found its grooves and edges intriguing to look at; however, like many six- year-olds, even the most interesting things lost their novelty after five minutes. My tooth soon became nothing more than a magical talisman that summoned the tooth fairy's monetary gift-giving.

My interest in dentistry was sparked, not in childhood play, but as an adult searching for her path in life. By my sophomore year in college, I still didn't have a clear sense of the road I should take. A fondness for working with my hands combined with medicine being a common choice among my science-loving peers led me to volunteering in the ER department. However, after years of volunteering at a hospital back in high school, I wasn't convinced that it was right for me, While I loved having the opportunity to connect with the patients, bonding with them over life-long dreams or cute grandchildren, I felt that there was an element missing. Thus my search continued.

The end of sophomore year brought a set of new lens to my career search. I had greatly valued the kinship and camaraderie that my Sponsor or "hall parent" provided during my freshmen year, and it inspired me to become one as well to pass forward my appreciation. I reached out to the intimidated freshmen, baked brownies on their birthdays, listened to their academic and emotional tribulations, and shared mine so they could be comforted knowing they weren't alone. What started out as a volunteer service, however, soon evolved into invaluable relationships that I built with my Sponsees ("hall-children"), convincing me that I wanted a career where I could interact with people to build long lasting bonds. It then dawned on me that dentistry could be the ideal profession as it appeared to contain the missing element. I decided to confirm this hunch through shadowing.

Dr. Tuttle was one of the general dentists who welcomed me into his practice with open arms. I admiringly observed him perform surgical procedures with the precision and efficiency one would expect after 40 years of experience. I saw his ability most clearly when he was treating a woman complaining about a chronic discomfort in her back molars. After a brief look in her mouth, Dr. Tuttle said, "Alright, let's see what I can do," and reassuringly patted her on the shoulder. His years of experience shined through as he was immediately able to diagnose the roughness of the filling performed by a previous dentist which impeded the patient from biting down correctly. When he finished, the woman was delighted that the soreness was gone! I realized how emotionally rewarding it could be for a dentist to instantaneously relieve a patient's dental pain which may have been persistently plaguing her for months.

Besides Dr. Tuttle's expert treatment, I also noticed and greatly appreciated how highly he regarded the psychological comfort of his patients. He showed me that an outstanding dentist not only repairs teeth but also calms nerves. This care strongly evoked the memory of my Sponsor experiences and confirmed that dentistry is my true calling because I value connecting with people on a personal level to foster a sense of comfort and welcoming. I found in dentistry the element that was missing in my hospital experience. In dentistry, I *can* have the pleasure to build long-lasting relationships with patients. What's more, I can do so in an environment which I feel is more conducive to doing my best work.

I am confident that I will both love and thrive in dentistry as I have enjoyed the hands-on component of research since my freshman year in college. My four years of pipetting into miniscule-sized gel wells and delicately picking E. coli colonies have furthermore given me a head start to acquiring the strong, steady hands that I know will be important to possess as a dentist. While the shape of teeth may not have been what initially drew me to dentistry, my shadowing experiences ignited my passion for the intangible benefits of this profession. With his sincerity and kindness, Dr. Tuttle has many patients who have followed him for over 30 years because of the strong connections he has built with each of them. I look forward to recreating those types of relationships between myself and the community and improve the oral wellbeing of each and every one of my future patients.

* * *

Commentary:

This essay takes a common approach by walking readers through how the author came to choose dentistry. For all experiences mentioned, applicants should be sure to not only exposit what happened but what it taught them— this author's nuanced lesson about patient comfort is a great example. Such a detail sets this essay apart for application readers who often are dentists themselves. The author further strengthens her position by showing how her past experiences set her up to perform well in this particular part of a dentist's job, as well as the more technical and scientific aspects. All this paint a picture of a candidate who is mature, relatable, and competent— exactly what every school wants their admitted students to be. —Dr. Liu

Author Bio:

- Lily Zhuang
- Pomona College, Molecular Biology, Class of 2014
- University of California Los Angeles, Class of 2019
- "I took a gap year because I needed that last senior year's grades to help raise my GPA after not doing too well in the first two years. This was a scary decision because my immediate and extended family pushed for going straight to dental school after graduating. Looking back, I don't regret this decision as this gave me the time to become a more competitive applicant with a satisfactory GPA, a 23 on my DAT, time to reflect and write my personal essay, and go on interviews without worrying about missing school. Going straight in is great, but there's no shame in taking a gap year. Take that year to find yourself, to decompress from working hard in undergrad, and to prepare yourself for one of the toughest four years of your lives. (Feel free to contact me at *zhuangjieyi@yahoo.com* if you have questions about dental school or the application!)"

15. MARC'S ESSAY

My intentions after graduating high school were to use my fascination with science to improve the health of others. I initially thought the best way to go about this was to start working my way towards a career as a nurse. After shadowing a nurse, I determined that career path wasn't for me. I was suddenly unsure of what I wanted to do with my life, I was only still sure of my love of science and desire to help others.

I had never put much thought into being a dentist until my family switched dentists, and I met Dr. Nowicki. His passion and enthusiasm for the dental profession inspired me to start a career in dentistry. After my first appointment, I asked to shadow him. While I was shadowing, I got to see first- hand how he has affected the lives of each and every one of his patients. Whether he relieved a patient of a toothache, or placed veneers on a patient so she had a beautiful smile for her wedding, his work has had a lasting impact on people's lives. I also got to see how he has built a relationship with all of his patients. I have always been a "people person", and I really enjoy working with the general public. It is my goal to make an everlasting positive impression on everyone I meet, and I know dentistry will help me fulfill that desire.

While I love the social aspects of dentistry, I didn't find out how much I truly enjoyed the field until after I earned a position as a dental assistant. I started assisting this summer for a group dental practice at multiple locations, and I absolutely love it. While I was shadowing Dr. Nowicki I saw how hands-on dentistry was. But it was not until I made my first temporary crown for a patient that I discovered how rewarding it is to create a functional "sculpture" for a patient. Another aspect of dentistry that I love is the challenge of managing your time. It's exciting to me knowing I have to develop radiographs, seat a patient, and run the autoclave, all while maintaining the highest quality of patient care. I look forward to the day, I have to do a crown delivery, while another patient is getting numb, and I have an exam to do for my hygienist. Each day at the office is action-packed and I wake up excited to go to work each day. I've heard it countless times, that if you find a job you love, you'll never work a day in your life. I have found that with dentistry.

Helping others has always been a passion of mine. Relieving someone of a burden is very rewarding to me. When I volunteered with my church's youth group at the Capuchin soup kitchen we relieved people's burden of hunger. The heart-felt gratitude I received pushed me to be even more active with my youth group while I was in high school. Another way I like to help others is through education. I was given the opportunity to be a teacher's assistant for both an anatomy and physiology lab, and a general chemistry lab for Oakland University. I thoroughly enjoyed every minute I had teaching the student's and helping them learn the material. I have also found I can fulfill my desire to teach through dental assisting. When I am working, I get to educate the public about oral hygiene, and it's benefits. I know that as a dentist I will have much more knowledge to share, and I will be able to help my patients even more.

Life is full of challenges that we must each go through. Going to university, and earning a higher education has not come without its challenges. The most significant burden to me was the financial cost of a higher education. In order to face this burden I have maintained employment throughout my entire college career. Unfortunately having to work took away from my time to volunteer. It also took away time I had to study, and earn the highest grades I am capable of; however, it did teach me many life lessons. I learned time-management, developed a strong work-ethic, and critical thinking. Overcoming the challenge of being able to afford a higher education has built my character in such a way that I feel I am a more compassionate, humble, and open-minded individual. I know these traits will help me thrive in dental school, and I am very excited to begin a career in dentistry.

* * *

Commentary:

Solid essay. I liked how this applicant has extensive exposure to dentistry from working as a dental assistant. I also liked his honesty about limited finances and stress over cost of school. By juggling part time work all through college; you get the sense he is a hard and responsible worker. Two critiques: The declaration "I have always been a 'people person', and I really enjoy working with the general public" comes across as vague and bragging, and I wish it was shown rather than told. Second, I'm not sure that this intro paragraph is the most engaging way to begin; perhaps it is an explanation why the applicant has more nursing than dental experiences. —Dr. Lian

Author Bio:

- Marc Huetter
- Oakland University, Biology, Class of 2014
- University of Michigan School of Dentistry, Class of 2019
- "I decided I wanted to be a dentist halfway through my undergraduate degree. After working many customer service jobs to pay for my undergraduate degree, I took a summer off to devote to studying for the DAT. I did very well on the DAT to compensate for my average GPA (3.3). After the DAT, I worked as a dental assistant until matriculating into dental school."

16. MARIAM'S ESSAY

Sitting at a table surrounded by faces, clipboard in hand, I quickly skimmed the first page of the experimental protocol my team and I had written. We were about to have our final meeting before clinical trials began for a revolutionary periodontal treatment my mentor had created. In the moments before we began to explain our experiment to a room full of dentists and hygienists, I reflected upon the long journey that had led me to this to this place. Halfway around the world, from Boston College to Cornell and Harvard, and from microbiology laboratories to professional offices, I could finally appreciate how the aggregate of my experiences had shaped my path to dental school and prepared me for my formal training.

Growing up with a father who is sixty-one years older than I am, I found myself shouldering domestic responsibilities at a young age. After he suffered a bleeding aneurysm while I was in high school, I had to forego my typical after school activities to begin caring for him. Burdened with neurological deficits from his episode, I had to assist him with tasks both big and small. I did these things begrudgingly at first, but soon I began to cherish the time I spent with him. What had first been sacrifices became acts of compassion and love as my patience and maturity deepened over the months of his recovery. It was during this time that I first became drawn to healthcare where I felt I could make a tangible and immediate impact on people's lives when they needed it most. Science classes at school suddenly took on new meaning, and I slowly saw my future as a healthcare practitioner come into focus.

Guided by this desire to care for others, I began researching under Dr. Hatice Hasturk at the Goldman School of Dental Medicine as a sophomore in high school. Under her guidance, I studied the connection between periodontal and cardiovascular diseases, and the influence of oral care on systemic health. What had started as a vague desire to help people quickly took shape - I began developing a passion for dental medicine. I continued dental research four years later when I became a research assistant at the Forsyth Institute in Cambridge, Massachusetts. It was here that I delved into the formation of oral microbiota, witnessing their spatial organization in plaque and tongue samples through spectral imaging and linear unmixing. It was here that I first saw *Corynebacterium* bordered by *Fusobacterium* and *Streptococcus*, and where I watched with amazement and fascination as corncob structures flourished from the coaggregation between *Fusobacterium* and other species. My summer research at Forsyth was transformative, so much so that it called me back during my Junior year. Though I was nervous to attend my third university, I knew that the classes I would take and the research I would engage in at Harvard would further prepare me for dentistry. Each day my love and knowledge of microbiology grew like the microorganisms I observed, quietly urging me to make sense of the relationships between the bacteria under my microscope and the billions of mouths in which they reside.

Determined to bridge the chasm between laboratory research science and clinical practice, I took a job working alongside prosthodontist Jonathan Levine in his company GloScience. Dr. Levine is changing how technology impacts dental care with a product that will one day streamline periodontal disease management. As an assistant researcher in the clinical trials, I've also had the opportunity to become involved with Foundation Rwanda, which provides holistic oral health for women and children affected by the 1994 Rwandan genocide. This is a cause I feel very strongly about after witnessing firsthand how profound the global disparities in oral health can be during an outreach trip to Hashtpar in Iran, a small settlement five hours north of Tehran. Seeing underserved individuals in such profound dental need inspires me to further my studies, my research, and my clinical skills so that I might one day have the opportunity to provide patients with an invaluable service. The path to dental school has not always been straight or clear, but I am eager to continue following the compass that has brought me to this moment - my unwavering desire to work for, dedicate myself to, and pursue dentistry no matter what it requires.

* * *

Commentary:

This applicant has a very mature voice. Her essay nicely references her impressive-sounding research background and volunteer projects without bragging or listing. One particular strength is how she weaves diverse details of her personal life that on the surface have nothing to do with dentistry (such as father being so much older than them, having to shoulder domestic responsibilities, interest in microbiology) into a coherent and interesting life story, showcasing the applicant as personable, thoughtful, hardworking, and a critical thinker. —Dr. Dragan

Author Bio:
- Mariam Zade
- Cornell University, Biology, Class of 2016
- Columbia University College of Dental Medicine, Class of 2020
- "A passion for science led me to my involvement in research during my 4 years in undergrad. During my junior year, a research position in the field of dental medicine influenced my switch from applying to medical school to dental school. Shortly after, I became more involved in the pre-dental club and began to shadow dentists around my college campus. Working with a dental related foundation solidified my choice in applying to dental school."

17. MICHELLE J.'S ESSAY

I do not like bicycles. Over the years, my subconscious has worked hard to suppress my last memory of riding a bicycle. However, at the word "bicycle," I flash back to age 13, flying down a sidewalk, frantically trying to decipher how the brakes worked before I could barrel into a new homeowner's human-sized clay vase. I skirted the vase by mere centimeters and managed a graceful stop by colliding into a very helpful tree. Needless to say, I haven't ridden a bicycle since.

While shadowing, I met John, who was passionate about the very thing I feared. John was undergoing a gingivectomy to expose the subgingival margin of a vertical fracture. He had been hit by car while riding his bicycle to work, resulting in serious fracturing of both central incisors and a mangled left forearm. For the past 4 months, he had been seeing a physical therapist for his arm and a series of dentists to fix his smile.

After observing the surgery, I found my thoughts returning often to John's case as the weeks went by. His case gave me occasion to consider everything I love about dentistry. The first is the opportunity to build strong relationships with patients. As a dentist, I would not only be able to follow patients like John from diagnosis to treatment but also keep track of their dental and overall health for years to come, far beyond the completion of their initial treatment.

Secondly, I am astounded by the bounty of solutions to each dental ailment, particularly since more solutions are continuously being devised as dental technology advances. Even in John's case, he had multiple treatment options available in restoring his fractured teeth— root canal treatment followed by a crown, or extraction followed by single tooth implants. Both options would have a similar prognosis. Additionally, as dental technology advances, even more options are being made available to patients. I believe discussions with patients to help them make the better choice in treatment empower patients to take control of and be involved in their own dental health. The freedom of choice would placate the fear of dental visits that plague many patients, eventually encouraging more visits to the dentist. With these open and honest discussions, I hope to educate patients about the importance of preventative dentistry and oral hygiene, thereby increasing the overall health and longevity of the patient and the health of the community as a whole.

Finally, as a dentist, I would always be able to continue my education. In the words of my personal hero, Malala Yousafzai, "[education is] a precious gift," and one that I will always be grateful for. Continuing education is crucial not only to expand my skill set but also because I aspire to be an inspiration for the new generation. I believe dentistry would be a fantastic medium through which I can experience lifelong growth and learning, particularly in a field teeming with new innovations. As a female dental professional, I hope to be a strong role model to young women by teaching classes and mentoring those who aspire to pursue a career in health sciences.

As for John, I ran into him weeks later in the elevator. During our slow descent, I asked how his treatment was going. In his response, he flashed me a delighted smile that put his beautiful new teeth on full display. I then noticed a bicycle lock clipped to his backpack and felt compelled to ask.

"Are you still riding your bike, even after going through all that?"

John cheerfully nodded. "Yeah, I still love it."

I was inspired that his providers were able to help John overcome such trauma. He can continue doing the activities he loves without his fractured teeth constantly reminding him of his painful experience. I had finally seen with my own eyes the huge difference that dentists can make in the lives and happiness of their patients, and I felt my conviction for dentistry grow. Because of cases like John's, I know that dentistry is my true calling. As we parted, I had the passing thought that maybe the next time I see a bicycle, I'll give it a try. I'm confident I can do it, just as I am confident that I will flourish in the dental profession, regardless of any rough weather or bumps in the road to come.

* * *

Commentary:

This essay does a fantastic job weaving an engaging narrative with what the author finds appealing about dentistry and wants to achieve within it. Many applicants shadow and volunteer because they're required, but this applicant shows that she was paying attention not only to a specific patient she met while shadowing, but also to the various aspects of clinical dentistry and how they intersected with the patient's life. By mentioning by name specific treatment options for this patient as well as specific issues and trends within dentistry, she shows a good grasp of the profession beyond the superficials one generally sees in a personal statement. The strong storytelling, including use of quoted conversation, is memorable enough that it all but masks this essay's single weakness: it tells us little about the author's own accomplishments and experiences. To make room for this, the author could have condensed the first and last paragraphs. —Dr. Liu

Author Bio:

- Michelle Jang
- University of California Los Angeles, Biology, Class of 2014
- University of Michigan School of Dentistry, Class of 2020
- "While working towards my bachelor's degree, I decided to pursue dentistry late during my junior year. Therefore, I took two gap years. During this time, I enrolled into additional courses to fulfill my remaining requirements, took the DAT, prepared my application, and worked and shadowed in various dental offices to expand my experience and understanding of the dental field. Throughout my undergraduate career, research, and work, I was blessed with a strong support system as well as several key mentors whose guidance was crucial to getting me where I am today."

18. MICHELLE P.'S ESSAY

The mechanism of a 35mm motion picture camera has changed very little in the past century. Based on a sewing machine, it has the interior beauty and complexity of a mechanical clock. These simple parts coming together precisely, rhythmically, and seamlessly are so elegant that one may forget that only a minor error in the mechanism can completely halt its function. As with the occlusion of the teeth, a minor change can lead to a cascade of problems. One year ago, I left my job as a camera assistant working on movies, television shows, and commercials, to pursue my goal of becoming a dentist.

As a camera assistant, I found joy in being part of and managing a team, mentoring young camera assistants, and troubleshooting frequent mechanical problems with cameras. Although I was enthusiastic about many aspects of my job, I realized that I wanted to spend my career interacting with and making a positive impact on the community around me. As a result of my experiences at work, volunteering, and with some powerful role models, I am confident that dentistry is a great fit for my talents and passions.

When I first began considering a career change, I went to see my dentist regarding some incessant pain in a lower molar. Over the next few months I saw my dentist first extract the problem tooth, then install an implant using the most fascinating tools and materials I had ever seen. While watching him, I couldn't help but draw comparisons with my experiences in the film industry, repairing and maintaining camera mechanisms. As I studied him managing and interacting with his team of assistants, I realized that dentistry was a career which combined my passion for working with my hands, with my love of managing a team, as well as my desire to interact with the community around me.

In addition to experiences with work, I have had wonderful role models who have been kind enough to give me advice and provide an example of what I hope to be one day. As a volunteer in the dental department at East Valley Community Health Center, which provides health care to low-income individuals, I have had the rewarding experience of assisting many talented, dedicated dentists who serve a community severely in need. Recently, we extracted three of a woman's remaining six teeth. In addition to the discomfort she was feeling with the infected teeth, she felt nervous just being in the office. She was a Spanish-speaking patient and, despite the language barrier, I did my best to comfort her. Dr. Winslow, the dentist I was assisting, has spent the last several years learning Spanish for this very reason. He was able talk with her directly about the procedure, which clearly made her feel more comfortable in the unpleasant situation. This exceptional effort for the sake of his patients is just one example of how the dentists at East Valley positively impact their community, a model I hope to embody through my own practice one day.

The experience of being a post-baccalaureate student, a full decade older than many of my classmates, has been a rewarding one. As a camera assistant, I took time to mentor several young people and helped start numerous careers, by sharing my knowledge of the equipment and guiding them on how to be effective team members. Over the past year, I have enjoyed the opportunity to learn from my fellow classmates as I transitioned back into life as a student, and in return have shared my experiences in the professional world with them. I hope to continue this as I move through my career in dentistry by mentoring and teaching future dentists.

In addition, the opportunity to approach classes in a more focused and mature way over the past year has been a gift. Effective study habits, which I only developed later in my undergraduate studies, have come naturally to me over the past year and have revealed my true potential as a student of the sciences.

I have invested a great deal of thought and time researching my decision to become a dentist. Through an array of experiences as a camera assistant, volunteering, and my post- baccalaureate program I know that I can thrive in dental school and will enjoy an interesting and fulfilling career as a dentist.

* * *

Commentary:

The stories about working as a camera assistant in the film industry set this applicant apart from more traditional applicants, and it is a smart angle to take in the essay. I appreciate the author's transparency regarding a career change decision and the reflective thoughts about a dental career; admissions officers expect a non-traditional applicant's personal statement to address this question. The essay nicely conveys her fascination with the intricacy of dental procedures, supported by the anecdote of volunteering in a community health center. I get the sense that the writer brings many life skills to the table and would be a collaborative and engaged peer in dental school. —Dr. Kuhn

Author Bio:

- Michelle E. Piasecki
- New York University, Film & Television Production, Class of 2008
- University of Los Angeles School of Dentistry, Class of 2020
- "Changing careers felt like a difficult and risky thing to do. My undergrad GPA was not particularly competitive and going back to school after almost a decade away from the sciences was tough at first. I knew I had to give it my all in my post-bacc year and try my best to frame my unusual background in a positive light on my application. To a lot of people the connection between cameras and dentistry isn't initially clear, so I thought it was important to prove to admissions committees that my seemingly unrelated background was actually a perfect fit. I owe a lot to the many mentors who read this and my husband who painstakingly read draft after draft, even if the only change was a semi-colon exchanged for a comma."

19. MIRISSA'S ESSAY

Curiosity got the best of me at a young age. Sure, I wanted to understand how things worked. I spent hours in second grade building Lego models fashioned after the architecture in my collection of *Redwall* books. But what I mean is that curiosity *really* got the best of me: it got my new, "permanent" front tooth.

At the age of seven, seeking my father's aid to troubleshoot the Nintendo, I decided to knock on the outdoor window rather than the door, curious to find a new way to gain his attention. I engineered a mountain of plastic chairs, climbed to the window, and opened my eyes moments later with my head on the concrete and blood in my hands.

What had I done? One of my two only permanent teeth, and my front tooth at that, had fallen out of my mouth! I began to cry out of sheer panic of seeing so much blood, and, unsure of where to go with a lost tooth, my dad rushed me to urgent care with my tooth delicately placed, roots and all, in a jar of milk. Finally, Dr. Moore, a dentist I didn't even know, rushed to his office in his flannel pajamas to restore my tooth to its original position. Even though he was exhausted, he left me with a photograph of my restored laughter as a keepsake of that night.

Certainly, most children would not find a dental visit inspirational; and, I would not say the sound of the drill or the constant nagging to floss my teeth greatly influenced my view of life. But that night, Dr. Moore inspired in me a desire more impassioned than words can express: a yearning to make a difference in the world through individual smiles.

The mouth is a fascinating portal into the human body, and at the age of seven, I was only just discovering how truly incredible that portal is. Each tooth is so intricately shaped, pleading for the precision and foresight of an artist's hand with every filling. As a potter molding clay in my free time, a jeweler and origami hobbyist working delicately with my hands, I can't help but adore the intersection of art and science that is dentistry.

But, what truly keeps my passion for dentistry alive is not only the potential to help people or the creative calling of the tooth, but how forcefully this creative ability to help others is rooted in health science. A simple lesion can mask an infection disintegrating the underlying bone. That bone is a chemical masterpiece with the strength to support a human body, but the weakness to succumb to one's own immune system. In that same region, the peripheral nervous system excites rapidly firing action potentials to signal the damage to the central nervous system, while the circulatory system acts as the shuttle through which the immune response is met. The mouth is the entrance to health, pain-free smiles, and even creativity, and my curiosity to understand its scientific intricacy with growing detail has incessantly flourished.

Even the ultimate curiosity alone, though, could not instill the level of passion for dentistry that awakens me each morning and nourishes me each day; and actually, as an ill child, I had to call this curiosity into question. Lying helplessly in a hospital bed with doctors condemning me to a nursing home for life, I faced a premature existential crisis: is curiosity reason enough to join forces with the very health professionals who are giving up on my health? I awoke each morning with Reflex Sympathetic Dystrophy spreading throughout my body and the pain of being stabled by flaming knives leaving me begging my mother and doctors to not give up. I was "too sick to treat," viewed more as a purple-legged liability than as a patient. To say I was angry at the medical response would be an understatement. Yet, in remission, no anger could outweigh the joy of painlessly hugging my father. No experience, from tirelessly starting a youth resiliency program to cleaning blood off an excavator as a dental assistant, could diminish the passion and determination that grew from my illness to not only spread pain-free smiles, but to be the empathetic medical professional I desperately sought.

Fourteen years ago—before even illness introduced me to health sciences—Dr. Moore did much more than inspire laughter from a frightened child. While my tooth did finally have to be removed, the direction in life that Dr. Moore provided, the inspiration to pursue a career in oral health—a field that truly delves to the medical underlying of a surface smile—has never and will never be yanked out of me.

* * *

Commentary:
She does a great job of highlighting the relationship between herself and an inspirational mentor leaving us with a great message—inspiration strikes when we least expect it! What I love about this piece are all the ways that she highlights the core qualities of a successful dentist. The author takes her essay one step further by highlighting relationships between medicine and dentistry, and it is clear that she recognizes that dentistry is not an isolated field. I like how positive the author comes across when sharing her mental struggles with a medical condition, and it appears that she is always up for figuring out how to overcome life's roadblocks. —Sangita Murali

Author Bio:
- Mirissa D. Price
- University of Colorado Denver, Biology (Minors in Chemistry and Leadership Studies), Class of 2014
- Harvard School of Dental Medicine, Class of 2019
- "When I was ten, a doctor said I would live in a nursing home, confined to a wheelchair, crippled by pain. Instead, I pursued pain-free smiles, founding a nonprofit aimed at enhancing self-efficacy in youth; working as a dental assistant in my gap year between college and dental school; and conducting dental biomaterials research to enhance the aesthetics and efficacy of composite restorations. Now, as a 2019 D.M.D. candidate and aspiring pediatric dentist, I have the honor and gift of living each day in the pursuit of spreading pain-free smiles. You can stay in touch with my writing and my dental journey at *https://mirissaprice.wordpress.com/* and follow @Mirissa_D_Price on Twitter or Facebook. Good luck and great smiles on your journey!"

20. MONICA'S ESSAY

I could feel the sharp pain of the needle as the local anesthetic was applied. I found myself eager to find out what came next, wishing I could see this procedure from a different perspective. It was time for general anesthesia and before I knew it I was out cold. I woke up with a bulging lower lip, numb tongue and missing my wisdom teeth. This eagerness I experienced during my procedure later escalated into my passion for dentistry.

I was born in Dubai, United Arab Emirates but I moved to and lived in Egypt until I was five, which is when I moved to the United States. Transitioning from speaking Arabic to English was a struggle; however, even though it took time I became proficient in English and I also managed to stay fluent in Arabic. My goal is to be able to communicate with immigrants that are not able to speak much English yet, so I can help them get appropriate dental care.

Throughout my life I've enjoyed the little details in large things. Like many young girls, I used to think I was going to be a fashion designer. My favorite hobby was sitting and working on a single sketch of an outfit for hours. Detail was everything to me, and it would never be good enough until it was perfect in my eyes. Eventually, I grew out of the fashion designer mindset, and I focused on sketching things that were in front of me. I made sure to pay close attention to the small things, as I realized correcting all the little flaws added up to a better picture.

Dentistry has been in my family for some time. My dad was a dentist, and worked in a dental lab. I always enjoyed going to the lab with him and sitting for hours watching everyone in the lab working on various things; whether it was tinkering with crowns or working on reconstructing a set of dentures, I loved it all. My father gave me one of my most cherished gifts, a large blue plaster model of teeth. I use to open up the model and use my dad's instruments along with extra crowns he would bring home and pretend that I was a dentist. To this day, I still have one of the porcelain coated gold crowns. This "toy" turned out to foreshadow my future career.

I decided I wanted to be able to play with those toys for the rest of my life. I began to shadow many general dentists in order to get a feel for the career. Being in Dr. John Haley's office kept me excited and comfortable at the same time, to the extent that sometimes I would be unaware of the time that went by. I saw everything from cleanings and fillings, to infections and extractions, in the office and after seeing each procedure I wanted to be able to do them myself.

Dr. Haley saw the passion I had for dentistry and would quiz me periodically. To his surprise, I never got a question wrong. I watched was being done before me very carefully. The ultimate test was when he told me to perform a filling on an old model of teeth. Dr. Haley had me sit in his chair, use his instruments, and remove all the "decay" (which was an old silver filling in this case) and pick out a filling that matched the color of the teeth and carefully fill in and sculpt the tooth. Although rather difficult, he said I did exceptionally well for it being my first time.

After shadowing many general dentists, I decided to explore the more of what the dental field had to offer. My eyes were opened while shadowing Dr. Ralph Eichstaedt in oral surgery. My passion for dentistry was taken to a new level when I had the privilege of witnessing a wisdom tooth extraction. Previously, when I was getting my own wisdom teeth pulled, I had wondered about the procedure and wanted to watch the extraction being performed on my own mouth. Now that I was in the dentist's position, I was astounded by what was done. I was looking on from a third person point of view and observing the intricacies of the event in detail. Never would I have believed that the procedure that happened in my mouth was the one I was watching being performed in front of me.

When asked how I know dentistry is the right career for me, I simply smile and think of all the things that have led me to believe I am ready to enter the field. Knowing that I will be directly involved with bettering my patient's lives puts a weight on me, but I want to step up to the challenge. I know now, more than ever, that this is what I want to do and what I will strive to become.

* * *

Commentary:

The author ropes us in with a vivid, if jarring opening about their experience undergoing anesthesia to remove wisdom teeth. The author chronologically describes her journey towards dentistry. As is the case in medicine, many pre-dental students have a parent or relative in dentistry. Fortunately, the author avoids the error of solely referring to her experiences at her father's dental practice and shows she made an effort to learn from other general dentistry and specialty offices. Overall, this piece is successful in its personal stories, tone, and authenticity. — Dr. Chen

Author Bio:
- Monica Ghattas
- University of South Florida, Biomedical Sciences and Public Health, Class of 2014
- Tufts University School of Dental Medicine, Class of 2018
- "Most of my time in undergrad was spent making sure my GPA stayed pristine. I was also very involved with my church and volunteered through that almost every week. I was lucky enough to go on a Medical & Dental Mission trip to Mexico, which I think helped me stand out on my application. I also allocated a lot of time to shadowing. It is honestly the most important thing before even thinking of applying to dental schools. I used to think I wanted to go to medical school—so I shadowed and did an internship where I did hospital rounds in different departments. That was the best thing I did because it made me realize how much I did NOT want to be a physician. I knew I wanted to be in the healthcare field, so I decided to shadow dentists next: general, OMFS, Endodontics, etc. and I absolutely fell in love. Everything in dentistry made sense to me, and I would not have known that without shadowing!"

21. NISHA'S ESSAY

As I walked onto the unlit stage, I positioned myself into the first dance formation using only the jingling bells stitched onto the outfits of my dancemates as a guide. The audience cheered as the emcee introduced our team, but all I heard was my heartbeat throbbing faster and faster. Meanwhile, my dance mates and I exchanged a look of support. As soon as the curtain lifted, my nervousness almost immediately turned into excitement. I felt prepared for this moment. Months of perseverance were finally going to pay off. At first glance, my lifelong hobby of dance and my career choice of dentistry seem to have no connection. However, dentistry is a profession that demands similar fundamental values as dance: passion, dedication, and persistence. Dentistry requires the perfection of small details in order to accomplish the final product, as well as building trusting relationships with patients.

When I started shadowing Dr. Othman Qahwash in high school, I began appreciating the nuances of dentistry more. From tooth extractions to learning about dental implant surgery, each procedure piqued my interest about the profession. As I spent more time in the clinic throughout college, I found myself eager to apply what I had learned, such as by detecting caries on a radiograph. Apart from the technical aspects of dentistry, I also understood the importance of effective communication in building patient relationships. Once, an elderly patient came in after receiving improper treatment from a former dentist. She was frustrated and generalized that all dentists were inept. Dr. Qahwash calmly responded to this attitude with understanding and reassurance. After the successful outcome of her treatment, she claimed that this was one of her best dental experiences yet. For me, her happiness was a testament to how dentistry can provide rewarding interactions with patients. Dr. Qahwash's passion for oral healthcare resulted in meaningful treatments for his patients, inspiring me to further explore dentistry as a career.

During my second year of college, I participated in a dental mission trip to Panama in which volunteer dentists provided free dental care to under-resourced communities. I was astonished to see that around 300 patients came to the clinic on just the first day. As more families walked in, it became crucial to keep the treatment and education stations running smoothly. Although I mainly assisted dentists during routine procedures, I also spent time in the education workshop teaching children how to properly brush their teeth through the form of a song. I was happy to be providing the children with the skills to maintain their oral health. To me, teaching the children about preventive education was the most sustainable aspect of the program. During the mission trip, I was able to enhance my ability to think quickly, advocate preventive education, and positively impact a community. In the future, I hope to use the knowledge I gained in Panama to educate patients and help them gain an appreciation for their oral health.

In addition to doctor-patient interactions and preventive education, researching with Dr. Juliet Brophy in dental anthropology exposed me to some of the technical skills required in dentistry. I assisted Dr. Brophy by assessing the occlusal outline of teeth in various specimens of human ancestors found in Africa. We then analyzed the data to better understand the relationships of species in the human evolutionary lineage. Initially, digitizing each tooth was difficult for me due to the level of precision required. However, with time, persistently repeating the process allowed me to improve my detail attentive abilities, which is an important skill I can take with me to dental school. While working with Dr. Brophy, I was able to take the skills—critical thinking, precision, and perseverance—that I had refined in Dr. Qahwash's clinic and Panama and apply them to a laboratory setting.

The values I have learned from my experiences as a dancer, dental assistant, mentee, and volunteer have reinforced my career choice to become a dentist. I have witnessed and applied the passion, dedication, and persistence that dentistry requires. My attentiveness to detail, and my desire not only to treat but also educate, give me a unique and valuable approach to dentistry. After much thought and deliberation through the years, I am fully confident that dentistry is my vocation.

* * *

Commentary:

This essay does a great job at capturing the author's diverse experiences in life and in dentistry. With a very strong, vivid first sentence, she already captured my attention and desire to continue reading. One of the strongest aspects of this paper is the plethora of examples, followed by a short and purposeful description that shows connection to the field of dentistry. Don't tell a story or give an example and stop there; make it clear what conclusions the reader is supposed to draw. Furthermore, tying in dancing makes the applicant stand out because it helps show how she can contribute to a diverse dental school class. —Dr. Watts

Author Bio:
- Nisha Patel
- Loyola University Chicago, Biology and Psychology, Class of 2016
- University of Michigan School of Dentistry, Class of 2020
- "Hi, my name is Nisha! Dancing is my passion/favorite hobby, so in my personal statement I wanted to uniquely connect my love for the art of dance to my passion for dentistry. While writing your personal statement, remember that many other students may have had very similar experiences and that's okay! What is more important and makes you stand out is showing AND telling the admissions what you gained from those experiences. That's what makes you unique!"

22. NYLE'S ESSAY

Dentistry is like restoring and maintaining a vintage automobile. If the owner takes care of the car from the start, cleaning and the occasional checkup is all that is required. If the car is mistreated and neglected, further work must be performed to make it operational again.

Like the typical young boy, I always wanted to be like my father. As a hobby, he restores antique cars, so I spent much of my time out in the garage. His hobby became mine as time went on. There is no rulebook to the process of rebuilding cars from rusty shells into functional pieces of art. The utilization of tools, knowledge, and creativity is necessary in solving the puzzle of a restoration. With time, I have acquired the ability to solve such problems, which is a talent that can be carried over to a career in dentistry. I want to take the skills I have learned in the garage and practice them in a health care profession. However, my decision to choose such a career did not come directly from the garage.

Being that same boy with an unconscious desire to be like my father, I spent many summers at his dentistry practice, pleading to help around the office. I was anxious to learn what he did, so he put me to work. I began simply with filing charts and answering the telephone. My responsibilities increased as I became older with jobs such as developing x-rays and filling out insurance forms. He then ordered an assistant chair so I could gain a more hands on experience with the patients. It was this job that triggered my desire to become a dentist. I enjoyed the personal interactions and observing how someone can go from unrelenting pain to comfortably eating again. Every mouth was different, making the process to solve each problem a puzzle with no definite answer. I have the creative capacity and manual dexterity required to be a successful dentist. Much of my life has been spent honing these skills out in the garage.

Beyond creativity and manual dexterity, a high academic aptitude is also necessary in dentistry. I chose chemistry for my studies because it requires the ability to combine and understand other disciplines of science, such as biology, physics, and math. The problem solving and ingenuity required in chemistry is similar to that of dentistry. I have been successful in my chemistry endeavors, which has prepared me for the rigorous course work of dental school. I have pursued opportunities to work in an organic chemistry laboratory in a constant effort to learn more. Though I enjoy the research aspect, the lack of interpersonal encounters in a laboratory reassured me that dentistry is a better-suited career. I would like to take what I have learned as a good chemist and use it to become a great dentist. The difficult chemistry classes I have endured prove that I am willing and able to take my education to the next level.

Another important aspect of dentistry is possessing natural social skills. Being the president of one club and vice president of another, I speak to many people on a daily basis. I have been complimented for being approachable and always wearing a smile. With the high positions of a club come many responsibilities that only a true leader could handle. Remaining organized and willing to work hard are important features necessary to manage any organization. Both of the clubs I have directed throughout my undergraduate career have been successful and have grown considerably since taking the positions. To be an accomplished dentist, it is important to be capable of maintaining an office and staff alongside working with patients. My oral communicative skills and leadership skills will be assets to a career of dentistry.

Since the revelation of my desire to become a dentist, I have discovered other branches of dentistry. I spent the last month of high school participating in an internship with my orthodontist. This experience made me realize that there is so much more to the mouth than just teeth. Being the opportunistic person I am, I also turned an appointment to the oral surgeon into a learning experience. I only accepted local anesthesia so I could observe the extraction of my wisdom teeth through a mirror. My mother thought I was crazy, but I found it exhilarating.

In high school, I knew I wanted to be a dentist. This is an optimistic thought for a teenager, but my ambitions remained throughout my college career. My life experiences have prepared me for dental school and a career in oral health.

* * *

Commentary:

The examples from his life give the vivid impression of a young man who likes to tinker, to problem solve, and to be helpful, all positives traits admissions officers seek. Restoring antique cars is a unique hobby that makes him stand out and also lends credibility to his manual dexterity. The author does a nice job showing with concrete examples and observations how his dentist father inspired him to become interested in dentistry from a young age, not simply from familiarity. —Dr. Yang

Author Bio:
- Nyle Blanck
- University of Connecticut, Chemistry, Class of 2013
- University of Connecticut School of Dental Medicine, Class of 2017
- "The strongest aspect of my dental school application was my research in an organic chemistry lab. It resulted in a publication in a prestigious journal, which the dental school interviewers loved to ask about. Being a chemistry major, the biology portion of the DAT was very difficult for me because I did not have significant exposure to this subject. Interviewers also liked that I was president of the UConn unicycle club because it demonstrated that I have hobbies outside of academics. In dentistry, positive interaction with the patient is essential so admissions officers liked seeing I can relate to the people I am treating."

23. ROHAN'S ESSAY

As I enter the dental health clinic, I notice my peers looking grim in the waiting area. However, I take a seat and feel a profound sense of gratitude. Growing up, I did not always have health insurance. I still remember being twelve years old and hearing my father scream through the phone, "How do you expect us to afford that!" My parents were immigrants from India who were trying to make ends meet and health care, especially oral care, was not as high on their list of priorities. Fortunately, the few times I could meet with health professionals, I felt an intrinsic sense of trust—I knew I was in good hands. I want to pursue dentistry to inspire the same sense of trust in the patients I treat.

I am grateful to Tufts University for allowing me to explore health care through the lens of engineering. Much of my coursework involved working together with my classmates to solve problem sets and complete group projects. In my Chemical Process Principles class each group member, at times, would contribute parts of a solution to a complex problem. In some cases, I would initiate the solution, but someone else would have a more efficient strategy for moving the problem forward. Collaboration has allowed me to understand when to be assertive about my opinions and when to listen. It has developed my ability to communicate effectively and approach problems with a fresh perspective. I hope to continue to collaborate with my classmates in dental school, where we can work together to navigate the challenges inside and outside the classroom.

My Tufts education would not be complete without my extracurricular experiences. I have played bass guitar for a student-run jazz ensemble since my freshmen year; I am consistently performing at concerts, on and off campus. Performing music has pushed me to be more open and confident. Writing music and singing in front of crowds of people used to feel like a daunting experience. But the more chances I took to perform, the more comfortable I became with expressing myself to whomever I was playing for. I began to channel my personal experiences and thoughts into my compositions. I want to bring this sense of openness to my approach with patients because it is the best way I can build connections with them. Performing has taught me how to remain calm and think critically under pressure. Playing guitar also requires hand-dexterity, which I believe will be a valuable asset in dentistry. Overall, my experience in the jazz ensemble has led to significant personal development; it has made me more accessible, and solidified my ability to perform.

My work experience with the Student Teacher Outreach Mentorship Program (STOMP) has been another fundamental experience outside of my coursework. For STOMP, I design lesson plans and curriculum in order to teach kids about engineering. Growing up, I was lucky to have mentors who showed me the value of education. Through this program, I hope to serve as a similar mentor to the kids. The most fulfilling aspect of my work has been improving my teaching and learning abilities. After my first semester in the classroom, I quickly realized that the students who were getting the most out of my lessons were the ones who were willing to fail. I noticed these kids consistently asked more questions and were interested in their work for longer periods of time. In moving forward, I started to focus on cultivating a classroom environment where failing was encouraged. I went so far as to introduce myself every semester with an embarrassing story where I had failed. My goal was not to show I had been wrong, but rather to show I failed because I had taken a risk. It was not something to be ashamed of, but an opportunity for growth. Personally, I also began to notice when I was afraid of being wrong in my classes and made an active effort to remain engaged in my learning. I know there will be instances in dental school where I will feel lost, but I know my fear of failing will not inhibit me from taking charge of such situations.

Back in the waiting room, I am engaged in a conversation with the receptionist. "Rohan, the doctor is now ready to see you," the nurse announces to me as she approaches the reception desk. Right before I leave the waiting room I take a moment to imagine how it must feel to be the dentist who is working today. I can't help but feel excited by the opportunity to help and connect, to build and improve.

* * *

Commentary:

Worrying over cost of treatment is something all dentists have experienced from the other side of the counter. Telling the story from the candid voice of a child hearing his father's frustration is particularly emotional. He is able to sympathize with future patients about high costs of health care and is motivated to be in a position to help others. From there, it is a solid essay describing various examples of experiences and leadership AND what he learned from them. The snake bites its tail here, meaning the intro and final paragraphs come full circle with the same story. This is a common and effective essay structure. —Dr. Lian

Author Bio:
- Rohan Joshi
- Tufts University, Engineering Science and Music Composition, Class of 2017
- University of Connecticut School of Dental Medicine, Class of 2021
- "A lot of my extracurricular activities centered around music. I played in the jazz ensemble and other student-run bands all throughout college and high school. While it's important to build up your resume for dental school, I think it's equally important to develop yourself personally. For instance, I stayed on a farm to record an album with my band the summer before dental school. Advice for pre-dental students: Don't be afraid to deviate from the traditional path to dental school!"

24. ROSS'S ESSAY

Give me the tallest forward for the corner kick. I am a defender who desires a challenging path. Playing through injuries and running to the final whistle are a part who I am. Since I was four, I have had a love for the game. During high school, I would run myself for hours, practicing each play, and going for just one more mile. I made the varsity squad as a freshman. During my junior year, I earned a starting position for the Olympic Development team and a spot in the Capital Area Soccer League (CASL). The CASL practices were an hour and 45 minutes away. Coach held them three days a week. I endured a grueling preseason and the starting role as their center back. During the third game of the season, I tore my anterior cruciate ligament. This devastating blow to my soccer career forced me to look back and realize my potential out of the sporting arena.

I desired to find the same passion I had for soccer in my profession. So, I jotted down the soccer characteristics that had grasped me since I was young: team like environment, fast pace, practicable, requiring constant thought, and exciting. A few Internet searches later and two or ten serious talks with my ophthalmologist dad, I realized that I wanted to see dentistry from the other side of the mask. Dr. Chauncey West gave me this opportunity. Within the first three hours of work that day, I saw him lead a crew of dental assistants. I saw Dr. West bounce from room to room not only knowing the prognosis and procedure, but the patient's name and family. I saw him accept patient bills as his own knowing that it will help the patient more than hurt his practice. I saw patients tear in pain then suddenly tear for joy after just 45 minutes of work. After three hours, I was sold and I wanted more. The following years only solidified the concrete like grasp that held me that amazing day.

Aside from doing well in college, loving my classes, and taking the DAT, I was attracted to activities I felt would give me the intangibles that Dr. West and his colleagues seemed to posses. Freshman year I joined the UNC Triathlon Club. Even though repetitive movement of large muscle groups will not aid my argument for acute manual dexterity, this experience strengthened my understanding of the ingredients needed for a functional team unit. Unlike high school or club sports, we had no coach. We were a strong team of about 20 undergraduates and graduate students. I swam, biked, and ran miles around studying while helping out club fundraising so that we could send a select few to nationals in Arkansas. Come sophomore year, I was introduced to NC Missions of Mercy: an organization that provides free dental care for those who cannot afford conventional dental care. During the Fayetteville mission, I volunteered each day. My roles included: suction cup emptier, sterilizer, dental assistant, and heavy lifter. The hugs, tears, and repaired smiles I saw that day assured me that dentistry is my path to happiness. I stayed way past my shift ending time.

Junior year, I invested my time in the National Biological Honor Society (TriBeta), Substance Free Social Committee, and undergraduate research. TriBeta gave me the opportunity to volunteer for the Ronald McDonald house, Relay for Life, and food drives. The Sub-Free Social Committee was my outlet to give back to my student community. I planned banquets, movie nights, and dorm holidays, and I also led both semesters' large capture the flag events. For undergraduate research, I was fortunate enough to earn a histology position for the Conlon Lab, a lab that specializes in research of congenital heart disease. My objective was to characterize the histological architecture of a heart that was compound heterozygous for two transcription proteins. This research reassured me that I love working with my hands. A mouse's heart is roughly the size of a molar, and I was required to fix and section the heart into 10 *um* sections, so that I could image it for potential publishing. I care strongly about the lab's mission and histological process, but I missed the quick results that dentistry provides. This clarification, again, led me to dentistry.

I will offer dentistry the same drive and passion I had for soccer. I am motivated to provide exceptional patient care. I desire the responsibility that a dental education gives. I aspire to reinvest into my community, however large it grows, so I can give confidence, take away pain, and construct brilliant smiles.

* * *

Commentary:

This essay conveys a strong personality with abilities to overcome difficult moments and make the most of what is given at a certain period of time. With the sentence "I will offer dentistry the same drive and passion I had for soccer" the writer comes across as a sincere, hardworking, and well-rounded applicant. One weak point of the essay is the second paragraph; descriptions of his first shadowing experience are not particularly unusual or exciting, so it makes the conclusion that "After three hours, I was sold" overdramatic, probably not worthy of "passion." Most shadowing experiences are not life-changing events, so it's more realistic to analyze, like he does later in the essay, the logical aspects of shadowing and dentistry that appealed to him.
—Dr. Dragan

Author Bio:
- Ross Carroll
- University of North Carolina at Chapel Hill, Biology, Class of 2015
- Columbia University College of Dental Medicine, Class of 2019
- "I joined the biology honors fraternity, and they rarely did much. I did do a year of research at Frank Conlon's lab, which mainly consisted of me doing histology while trying to explain congenital heart disease and cardiomyocyte development and maintenance. It didn't feel like I did much when I compared myself to my classmates. Before college, I earned my Eagle Scout, worked as a host for a pizza restaurant, and played a bunch of soccer."

25. RYANE'S ESSAY

Ever since I was 11 years old, I've been committed to improving my health and understanding the science behind it. I eventually realized that I could turn my interest in science into a career and, at 27 years old, I discovered that dentistry was the career path I wanted. I considered various healthcare fields, but recognized that dentistry uniquely combined all the roles I love; I'd be an educator, community leader, scientist, artist, entrepreneur, business manager, and health provider. I knew I had found my passion.

I have come to define success as doing what I love. To achieve my definition of success, I realized that I needed to fully commit myself to dentistry. It was an exciting realization, but it required a path that was radically different from the path I was on. Nonetheless, I knew the hard work would be worth it - the five years I spent working in business taught me how to build lasting and meaningful relationships, but more importantly, it also taught me that nothing worth accomplishing ever comes easy.

To achieve my goals, I had to jump off the boat and swim against the current. As an Economics major at Colgate, one of the concepts I studied was opportunity cost; it's the cost associated with choosing one thing over another. The opportunity cost of leaving my career to pursue dentistry was significant: two years of tuition, as well as foregone salary, promotions and investment income. It was an expensive decision, and I didn't take it lightly. Ultimately, I decided that even though I wasn't unhappy with my career, life shouldn't be lived "not unhappily." Life is about finding your passion and having the courage to pursue it. I realized that the opportunity cost was irrelevant; the only cost that mattered was the cost of not doing what I loved. I had to dedicate myself to dentistry, and that's exactly what I've done.

One of the most impactful ways I've connected myself to the profession is by getting involved in organized dentistry through the American Student Dental Association. I've attended local and national ASDA events, built a personal network of dental students across the country, and I was one of only two pre-dental students to participate in the ASDA debate at the 2015 Yankee Dental Congress. By joining and actively participating in ASDA, I've learned a lot about dentistry's societal impact, as well as the current and future challenges it faces. My involvement has made me realize that, beyond being a proficient clinician, I want to be a leader in the dental field. I want to help drive change and be an integral part of moving dentistry forward as a profession. I'm honored that ASDA is also confident in my leadership potential; I was recently appointed to a National Pre-Dental Leadership position.

Beyond being a leader within organized dentistry, I've also shown recent and relevant academic excellence. At Colgate, I studied Economics because there was no Business or Finance major. I had no tenacious interest in economics, which proved a recipe for becoming an average student. My approach in my post-baccalaureate work has been entirely different. I've maintained a full course load while balancing volunteerism, tutoring, paid employment, and organized dentistry. I also founded and currently serve as President of my school's Pre-Dental Society. With less time on my hands now than when I was a Division-I student-athlete at Colgate, I've maintained a 4.0 GPA. Having a clear vision of what I want out of my future combined with a genuine interest in science has made, and will continue to make, all the difference.

Aside from my interest, commitment, and leadership, I also bring polished interpersonal skills and relevant business experience to the table. I spent five years learning how to control costs, grow profits and provide superior customer service. I was a top salesperson thanks to my ability to build connections and trust with people. At Enterprise, I was ranked #1 on the ME/NH performance matrix for 13 months. I also managed and was part of a team that achieved the #2 customer service score in the entire company.

I'm driven, determined, and excited to lead. Each day that passes brings me one step closer to realizing my goals. I don't know all the details of my future, but I do know it will involve dental school and being a respected and valued member of the dental community. My tomorrow is bright and exciting, and I can't wait to open my eyes and see what it looks like. I hope you're there.

* * *

Commentary:

This non-traditional applicant weaves a convincing and interesting tale about his journey to dentistry from amidst uncertainty of a career change. One meaningful example of learning about dentistry is his involvement with the American Student Dental Association and organized dentistry, something that relatively few pre-dental students pursue. In addition, the author clearly highlights his background in business and economics, from which he gained concrete skills that are translatable to dental practice. The tone is more determined and confident than most, with the final sentence being forward but not too aggressive. Being older than most applicants, this applicant comes across as mature, well-informed, and ready to jump head first into dentistry.
—Dr. Chen

Author Bio:
- Ryane Staples
- Colgate University, Economics major (minor in Educational Studies), Class of 2009
- University of Connecticut School of Dental Medicine, Class of 2020
- "I was a division I college athlete at Colgate, and that took up a lot of my time. When I graduated, I enjoyed a short but successful career in sales and management for five years before returning to school to pursue dentistry. When I did my post-bacc at University of New Hampshire for the dental school pre-reqs, I also became a tutor and even started the Pre-Dental Society. Having been an average student at Colgate, I really poured myself into my post-bacc studies and forced myself to get a 4.0 GPA - it can be done, I promise!"

26. SANGITA'S ESSAY

Amos delicately placed the two hand-drums on silk placemats in front of me. My eyes lit up with excitement, but as I began to play silence flooded the room. My hands clumsily patted the drum producing hardly anything one could call a purposeful sound. I was inadequately living up to my name, *Sangita*, which means *music*.

Within a few minutes, though, my fingers re-adjusted and figured out what they wanted to do, and Amos was impressed! "Usually students struggle for a few lessons!" he announced. I was pleased and thought that my experiences with playing the piano and violin may have contributed to my aptitude for playing the hand-drums.

By shadowing a general dentist, I learned that the manual dexterity required to play instruments bears a direct correlation to the skills required to be a dentist who must work with precision and exercise very fine motor control. Playing instruments, in addition to strengthening my coordination skills, has also allowed me to sharpen my concentration, enhance my listening skills, and promote my interpersonal skills. Through my interactions with a general dentist, I have found that these elements are crucial to providing high quality oral care which additionally attracts me to choose dentistry as my professional career choice.

In addition to my proclivity towards music, I have a great passion for research and have worked in genetics, cancer, and toxicology laboratories most summers since high school. These internships have fostered my interests in biochemistry and immunology, and my senior thesis in cognitive neuroscience additionally taught me how understanding a person as an individual influences health outcomes.

Early in the fall of 2011, I met Ms. Lewis (a pseudonym), a clinical study participant for my thesis exploring the relationship between vitamin D serum levels on cognition and white matter brain changes in Maine residents with Multiple Sclerosis. Ms. Lewis helped me realize that being a good health care provider entails more than knowing the pathophysiology of disease or knowing how to do the tests. In addition to a dosage schedule of vitamin D, she needed me to understand the emotional and psychological ramifications of her illness and what additionally is most important to her: every- day comfort. From shadowing, I have learned this is required of dentists too who not only need to understand the pathology of periodontitis, for example, but who must curb their patients' dental anxiety and understand how hormonal changes, medications, and illness like diabetes impact the individual. This extra measure of empathy is what turns a good health provider into a compassionate ally.

During my shadowing experiences, I also became increasingly aware of and impressed with the technical challenges that accompany dentistry and how overcoming these challenges change lives. One of the most fascinating and more complicated procedures I observed recently was one in which the dentist performed a six-unit dental bridge on a patient. The result of this procedure more than corrected the woman's decaying teeth. She gleamed with higher self-esteem and a greater sense of self-confidence. Just as an artist applies paint with deliberate and purposeful brushstrokes, the general dentist carefully altered the contours of the crown ensuring that it matched the original tooth exactly and in flawless accordance with the patient's bite. In addition to striving to be a compassionate ally to his patients, perfectionism is another shared attribute between the two of us.

In addition to playing instruments and conducting laboratory research, I have also played ice hockey, served my student body as class president, and tutored colleagues. These experiences have all contributed to my strong hand-eye coordination, manual dexterity, enthusiasm towards the biological sciences, affinity for leadership, and my desire to teach and serve others. Furthermore, these experiences have reinforced my aspirations to become a dentist where I can encourage people to engage in preventative health measures such as brushing and flossing that reap major benefits like preventing gum disease and maintaining both oral and overall health. In dental school, I look forward to synthesizing the skills that I have developed and the scientific knowledge I will gain to find my "rhythm" with treating patients and providing excellent oral care to the community.

* * *

Commentary:
This essay goes full circle with the theme of music and dentistry. She incorporates how her experiences as a pianist, violinist, and more recently drummer correlate with manual dexterity and teaches her about the rhythm of dentistry. In addition, the author has a host of interesting and vividly presented anecdotes ranging from an in-depth senior thesis research experience to clinical shadowing experiences, both of which underscore the empathy and human element needed as a healthcare provider. There is vivid and descriptive language, proving the author to be a capable writer.
— Dr. Chen

Author Bio:
- Sangita Murali
- Bates College, Neuroscience (Minors in Applied Mathematics and Public Health), Class of 2012
- Tufts University School of Dental Medicine, Class of 2018
- "The opportunity to improve a person's smile and self-confidence made dentistry a very attractive career choice for me. To make myself a competitive applicant, I devoted time to shadowing dentists, conducting research, and volunteering to provide much-needed oral health services in the community around me. Spending time with dentists who work with patients with various physical, medical, developmental, or cognitive conditions who may not easily receive access to dental care reinforced my decision to apply to dental school. I enjoy helping people and was excited to gain a heightened knowledge and skill set to make others feel comfortable."

27. SPENCER'S ESSAY

CRASH!! My attention explodes and re-focuses: "Dad!" My father is seizing violently in his seat, his eyes rolling to the back of his head. Just a moment ago we were reminiscing about our poor luck fishing today; now he is a firework of physiological fury. Terror...then lucidness falls. I immediately assess the situation and move: I clear the space, call 911, and, once he stops seizing, check his airways. My father is not breathing. I cautiously move him to the floor, lay him flat and tilt his head back—but still no breath. Again the dance of terror and subsequent clarity and calm; I *remember...*

"Never underestimate the power of a jaw thrust!" Dr. Mistry exclaims in the Honduran cloud forest. It is 2011, and I'm immersed in Operation Wallacea's month-long Medical Experiential Program. The birds are singing lustily as we trudge through the perilous forest, seeking direction like characters in a Golding novel. I ponder what Dr. Mistry has said. Could a jaw thrust really be that important? Of all the subject matter learned, from pre-expedition planning to tropical infections, *a simple jaw thrust?*

A barking dog outside wrenches my mind back to my father. Resolute, I reach down and grasp his posterior mandible and thrust it forward. *GASP!* He's breathing! *Good call, Dr. Mistry.* "Dad?" No answer —but his breathing seems to have steadied. I give him a soft pinch; encouragingly, he pulls away, proving he is responsive to stimuli. *Knock knock.* "It's open!" An officer barges hastily through the door, followed closely by EMTs who proceed to take my father to the hospital.

This radical experience notwithstanding, I realize that healthcare isn't always about saving someone's life; most of the time healthcare is about giving people new hope or attempting to better their lives. And this is reason enough to do it. Seeing the smiles on all the children's faces while we rebuilt a school's playground and health facility in Cahuita, Costa Rica last year was all the evidence I needed of the power of serving others. Albert Schweitzer once said, "Wherever a man turns, he can find someone who needs him." The realizations I made in Costa Rica—that serving others is a monumental privilege, that I am capable of both dramatic and subtle forms of health service—have solidified my desire to be a dentist.

**

Compassion is one of the most important qualities a dentist can possess. Dentists need not only to be skilled but also to have the ability to empathize with patients—as they say, people do not care what you know until they know that you care. World-class dentists also show tenacious drive and commitment to the craft; they possess a relentless desire to further both their skill sets and their fields of expertise. I have long considered myself a person of deep compassion and of deep respect for self- improvement, and am excited to apply these well-honed attributes to the dental profession. Above even these abilities, however, lie communication skills—the most imperative trait of any elite dentist. All the knowledge in the world will do you no good if you are unable to transfer your insights into the beneficial edification of others. Without terrific listening and articulation of expectations, it is not an exaggeration to say that irreparable harm can befall the crucial patient-doctor relationship. All of these characteristics—compassion, tenacity, and communication skills—are essential traits that every dentist should possess, and it is my unwavering belief that I possess each of them. They can, however, always be improved—and I am committed to seeing that they are.

The professional future I currently envision will undoubtedly be demanding and entirely rewarding. First, I plan to matriculate to dental school and obtain a placement to a highly competitive residency. Later, I intend to contribute time to Operation Smile; one day, in fact, I hope to create a similar organization to expand OS's impact. Through this and other projects, I see myself as an agent for positive change in the world community—and dental school is the imperative first step.

Today I am chasing down the dreams that at times in my life seemed so distant—dreams once seemingly suspended in the murky abyss of unfulfilled promise, far out of reach. However, through unvarnished perseverance, the distance that once appeared too far to fathom is now within my grasp. Whether this dream takes me abroad or back to NJ, I am ready to contribute—to make these dreams a reality.

* * *

Commentary:
The essay is written written and impactful. The emotional personal experience narrated in the first few paragraphs appears to be the source of this applicant's commitment to excellent patient care. The essay shows that he done significant reflection on the qualities necessary to be a good doctor. It shows vision and commitment to oral health care, seeing further than just clinical dentistry. My two recommendations are to try to connect the initial story to the end of the essay, and further explore into why specifically dentistry, rather than medicine in general. —Dr. Dragan

Author Bio:
- Spencer V. Meyers
- Quinnipiac University, Biochemistry, Class of 2012
- Columbia University College of Dental Medicine, Class of 2018
- "Greetings! I hail from the exotic land of New Jersey and completed my undergrad studies at Quinnipiac University. In college I completed research in synthetic organic chemistry, specifically stalling peptides and their correlation to antibiotic resistance. I played college baseball and started the Quinnipiac Chemistry/Biochemistry Club. I took two gap years after college to travel and really be sure that dentistry was in fact the field I wanted to be a part of. I have never been happier with a decision in my life!"

28. STEVEN'S ESSAY

I was born and raised in El Paso, Texas. This diverse city is situated on the border of New Mexico and the city of Ciudad Juarez, Mexico, where both my mother and fiancé were raised. I grew up with a strong sense of family, and through childhood experiences and participation in the youth orchestra, sports, school activities, and the church, developed a strong sense of community and a passion for helping others. During high school, I also developed a love for learning and a passion for science and the natural world, spurred on by my chemistry teacher Mr. Monsey, leading me to major in biochemistry. I knew as I entered college that I wanted to find a profession that would be both intellectually stimulating as well as put me in a position to serve the community, which has led me to pursue a career in dentistry.

I identify strongly with the Hispanic culture, a culture in which people are friendly and hospitable, even when faced with difficult circumstances. As a young child, I used to visit Cd. Juarez frequently to see my mother's side of the family, but was forced to limit these visits as Cd. Juarez experienced a surge of drug-related violence. The violence escalated to such a point that Cd. Juarez was rated by many as the most violent city in the world in 2010. It seemed like everyone had a family member or friend impacted by the violence, like my fiancé's best friend who lost her father to cartel members. I worried every day as my dad commuted across the border to work, hoping that he would be safe. The sense of fear and uncertainty that I had during this difficult time led me to rely more on others for support and emphasized the importance of community.

Even though the community around me was very strong when I was growing up, I still witnessed many social disparities. When driving in Cd. Juarez, you could be in an area with elaborate, sprawling houses one minute while 5 minutes later be in an area without paved roads and dilapidated buildings. It was difficult to watch children under 10 years old begging for money as I crossed the international bridge, as they were forced to bring home income for the struggling family rather than go to school. I also saw people working very hard at maquiladoras to bring home $50 a week. I felt moved by what I saw around me to help these people, and I knew I wanted my career to focus on having the most impact in the community as possible.

The summer after my freshman year in college, I asked to shadow my local dentist, Dr. Laws, as I was new to the area and was interested in his work. Dr. Laws graciously allowed me to shadow and more, eventually becoming a mentor to me. He showed me how I could apply my major, biochemistry, by understanding more of the tools that dentists work with and using the information to determine which one is best for the patient. I saw how his motivation for his work and human touch had a discernable impact on his patients. Many would come into the office apprehensive and fearful about their procedures and would leave happy and calm. This was the direct result of the friendliness of the staff and Dr. Laws' genuine caring for his patients. After several weeks, I came to the realization that my personality and skills were best suited in dentistry. Growing up, I knew I would enjoy working with my hands, as I would spend all day designing and building different toy figures. Dentistry is a great way to utilize this passion for creation, while also being diverse with its challenges. Another one of the biggest draws to me was the patient interaction. I was able to build a rapport with the patients, and saw how being a dentist allows the opportunity to see families often enough to build relationships, which is a unique experience.

While shadowing, I often saw patients unable to afford adequate care, which is something I would work hard to change as a dentist. I believe that everyone should be able to experience the same level of treatment, regardless of their financial status. My goal and main motivation to become a dentist is to go into underserved areas and provide first rate care, regardless of the financial implications. I know that to truly make a change in a community, one must do more than provide medical treatment, but also provide the means and education to make a lasting impact. I am committed to working with others to find long term solutions in underserved areas; I want to use the profession of dentistry to elevate others to a higher quality of life.

* * *

Commentary:

This is a solid personal statement that illustratively and honestly depicts the writer's upbringing and personal environment. It is successful in that he not only writes about his culture and witnessing the social disparities firsthand, but also elaborates on how these experiences shaped his thought process and motivation to give back to the same underprivileged communities. There are mature observations about the impact one can have as a dental professional on a community's health, and the author ends the essay with strong writing about his goals and desires to this end. It is clear that he would be a good addition to the dental class and bring a broader perspective and nuanced insights as expressed in this thoughtful piece. —Dr. Chen

Author Bio:

- Steven Cosgrove
- Arizona State University, Biochemistry (Minor in Business), Class of 2017
- University of Connecticut School of Dental Medicine, Class of 2021
- "While in college, I conducted biochemical research on the 3D-structure of membrane proteins. Although I enjoyed the research, I most enjoyed my time as a 4-year member of my college Habitat for Humanity chapter, where I was able to help my community while making strong friendships. I also was a Supplemental Instruction (SI) leader, which is a sort of peer mentor, as well as part of the Arizona Mentoring Society, which provided tutoring to elementary school students. For me, I found it was easiest to stay motivated by doing activities that made an impact on others, and helped me to get connected to others on campus."

29. THOMAS'S ESSAY

How do you get an aircraft turbine to remain above freezing at 17,000 feet using only 60 watts of heating power? Our professors were asking us for the impossible, yet we found options to provide the best possible outcome under the given conditions. The resulting gratification that comes from reasoning through a problem and executing the best solution engaged me in engineering while laying the foundation for my career in dentistry. For me, dentistry is an extension of engineering in that I can apply a diagnostic toolbox while developing personal relationships with patients.

Introduced to dentistry at just four years old, I endured numerous dental appliances including a palate expander, retainers, and a bluegrass appliance. I sat terrified as my general dentist detailed how an oral surgeon would detach my jaw to correct its alignment. Considering varying proposals from three other dentists, my parents and I opted for braces under the guidance of a thoughtful, caring orthodontist who recognized my fears and built a long-term, trusting relationship with my whole family. Four years later I looked in the mirror and was fascinated with how a few metal wires and rubber bands had transformed what once looked like a first grade art project into something Adrian Monk would be proud of. My interest was sparked. I value the vision, dexterity, and creativity of the work, the gentleness, transparency, and empathy imparted to patients, and the confidence the dentist is able to build in his patients.

Dentists follow an empirical process with their patients to engineer the envisioned results. However, while shadowing dentists, I saw that treatment is as much a social exercise as a technical one. Getting to know the patients was not only enjoyable but also necessary to provide the best treatment and comfort. In one case, when the dentist left the room while a dose of Septocaine took effect, Heidi, our patient, seemed anxious. I interjected with simple small talk about her job and family. I was taken aback, then humbled, when she told me about her husband's battle with Parkinson's disease and his uncommunicative doctor. I thought about how this might play into her treatment: her fears about under-communication and her stress stemming from her husband's health. How would this knowledge affect how Dr. LeClair administered her treatment and gave her guidance? Such moments confirmed my affinity for the challenge of balancing the finesse of working with tools as well as different personalities.

Studying engineering while pursuing dentistry has required me to build my problem-solving skills and given me the ability to apply them to different disciplines. Elected president of my pre-health fraternity, I needed to identify directions in which our members could grow and mature. Sitting in Starbucks for one-on-one chats with two-dozen new inductees, I learned that Amine wanted medical exposure through hands-on activities and Eva wanted to see alternative options for nursing career paths. They were all looking for more information about what lies ahead—very much what I observed in patients during my shadowing experiences and felt during my own treatment. To address the many ambitions of our members, some of the events I organized included a suture clinic led by the U.S. Army Medical Department and a forum with a nursing school alumna turned management consultant.

While the rules of science are available to provide guidance, sometimes you must also be resourceful. I was advised during my freshman year that, with my schedule, studying abroad would be nearly impossible. However, after considering the constraints to complete the mechanical engineering courses and the pre-dental requirements, I designed a plan which enabled me to go abroad while taking challenging courses that filled my requirements. By 2016 I will have graduated with a BSE in Mechanical Engineering, fulfilled all pre-dental requirements, studied in Hong Kong, and served as president of a fraternity. With commitment and perseverance, I have found a way to reach my goals.

Dentistry provides a vehicle for me to engineer solutions for patients while attaining the desired results and building personal relationships. It requires skill, creative thinking, and hard work. Even though the laws of science dictate that some things are impossible, I am committed to finding the best outcome given the conditions.

* * *

Commentary:
Even though every personal statement answers the same basic questions (Who are you? Why dentistry?) and covers similar ground (influential mentor, shadowing, hobbies), how one chooses to write certain sentences offers insights into different applicants' personalities. In this essay, the dominant qualities are that of critical thinking and problem solving ("For me, dentistry is an extension of engineering in that I can apply a diagnostic toolbox while developing personal relationships with patients." The applicant comes across as analytical, proactive, someone who likes to take charge.
—Dr. Yang

Author Bio:
- Thomas Hoopes
- University of Pennsylvania, Mechanical Engineering, Class of 2016
- Columbia University College of Dental Medicine, Class of 2020
- "My undergraduate education and hobbies were split between two focus areas of focus, pre-dental and engineering. On the pre-dental side, I dedicated most of my time to Penn's professional pre-health fraternity of which I served as president, and I loved being involved in the community service aspects of the fraternity and health field in general. In engineering, I worked for two summers doing clean room pipe flow engineering and project management, and I really enjoyed learning about the technical aspects of various industries such as manufacturing and automobiles. I get asked a lot about my choice between dentistry and engineering, but I always knew dentistry was my path and I just tried to get as much out of my other passion as I could before I committed to dentistry."

30. VICTORIA'S ESSAY

It was Christmas Eve in 2012 when I found myself with my mouth wide open, staring intently into my dentist's eyes behind his loupes. Earlier that week, I had developed a throbbing pain in my lower-left jaw that began radiating throughout my skull. An urgent call to my dentist, Dr. Ray Liu, landed me an impromptu appointment to extract my wisdom teeth. As I nestled myself into the dentist's chair, my brain brimmed with questions. Why was I experiencing such excruciating pain? Why were my wisdom teeth impacted? How long will this procedure take, and how much will this procedure cost? My thoughts probed such questions as I watched the reflection of Dr. Liu's scalpel pierce my swollen gums.

The quick whirlwind of events left a lasting impression on me. In particular, the surgery's complexities piqued my interest in oral health, so I began shadowing Dr. Liu. As I volunteered at his dental offices, I observed that Dr. Liu often conversed with his patients about their families, careers, and even statistics from the latest baseball game. Dr. Liu's willingness to connect with his patients' lives led me to realize that a successful dentist needs more than an interest and expertise in oral physiology – dentists must also cultivate strong patient-provider relationships. Over the course of one-and-a-half years, I developed a sincere appreciation for the immense compassion with which Dr. Liu treated his patients, and I longed to do the same.

At the University of Pennsylvania, my budding interest in the hands-on aspect of dentistry bloomed. As a sophomore, I participated in Penn's Dental Impressions Program where I waxed up central incisors, drilled an Ivorine tooth for an amalgam restoration, and hand-mixed alginate to produce an impression and pour a cast model. The Program was incredibly reminiscent of high school when I captained our Robotics Team. We similarly drilled, soldered, and handled power equipment in order to create a functional and aesthetically pleasing product. In addition to the Impressions Program, I recently observed fourth-year student dentists as they treated their patients from West Philadelphia, a traditionally underserved neighborhood. In shadowing both professional and soon-to-be dentists, the common theme that dentistry serves entire communities, and not just individual mouths, resonated within me. In fact, these experiences, coupled with my personal experiences at the time, furthered my interest to become a dentist and work for the underserved.

In accordance with one of my fundamental values, I strongly believe that people with privilege have the civic duty to work on behalf of those with less. In retrospect, this core tenet began defining my college career after my family did not accept me for 'coming out' of the proverbial closet. As a queer Asian woman, I realized that neither the heteronormative Asian community nor the Caucasian-dominated Lesbian, Gay, Bisexual, Transgender, and Queer (LGBTQ) community addressed the needs of over one hundred queer Asians at Penn. With this moral compass in hand, I was determined to serve the underserved. I brought together students, faculty, and administrators my sophomore year to establish a new student group called 'Penn Queer and Asian.' The mission of this organization is to raise awareness of intersectional identities. In the future, I hope to combine my experiences in student advocacy with my interest in dentistry to also become a patient advocate. Dentists possess unique social, political, and educational privileges, and I hope to become a dentist so that I can provide oral care and, more importantly, increased access to oral care to those who need it most.

Looking back on my wisdom tooth extraction, I realize now that the question I meant to ask my dentist was, "Why is this procedure happening *today*?" Reclined in the dentist's chair, I could not fathom why Dr. Liu willingly performed oral surgery on Christmas Eve, a day I expected most professionals to take brief respite. However, Dr. Liu's decision to prioritize an ailing patient's health resonated with my fundamental belief in serving those who are less privileged. For this reason, I know that a dental education will provide me with the skills to deliver oral care within the microcosm of a dental office and the macrocosm of the American healthcare system. Among the patients, procedures, and policies, my experiences thus far have affirmed my belief that dentistry is the perfect career for me.

* * *

Commentary:

I thoroughly enjoyed reading this essay. She has a strong grasp of what it means to form a patient-doctor relationship and to serve the underserved. Her definition of underserved is expanded through stories, demonstrating that everyone in a vulnerable situation is in need of support and a caring provider. The writer comes across as an inquisitive and reflective person. She is curious about the reason for wisdom teeth pain and reflects on the complexities that landed her in the dental chair on that specific day. In support of the writer's curiosity and interest in systems at-large, I found the story about establishing the Penn Queer and Asian group to be powerful. I get the sense that the writer is a change-agent and a valuable member of the community. —Dr. Kuhn

Author Bio:
- Victoria C. Chen
- University of Pennsylvania, Biology (Minors in Healthcare Services Management and Biological Basis of Behavior), Class of 2016
- University of California Los Angeles, Class of 2020
- "There existed the question of whether or not to disclose my sexual orientation in the personal statement, but since it is a large part of my identity and application, I figured I should. When it comes to applying, making sure that you feel not only welcomed, but also embraced at a school, is extremely important. I would recommend highlighting what make you unique as an applicant in your personal statement. This is your opportunity to showcase your strengths and passions, aside from numbers and demographics."

POSTSCRIPT

THANK YOU for reading this book. We would love to hear from you as you embark on your pre-dental journey!

Please email tips, advice, comments, or other inquiries to: dentalschoolessays@gmail.com.

Made in the USA
Coppell, TX
15 May 2022

77818790R00090